T0077699

NOT BY CHANCE

God's "Coincidental" Guidance of My Life

LYNN COCHRANE LEONARD

WESTBOW
PRESS
A DIVISION OF THOMAS NELSON

Copyright © 2010 Lynn Cochrane Leonard

All rights reserved. No part of this book may be used or reproduced by any means, graphic, electronic, or mechanical, including photocopying, recording, taping or by any information storage retrieval system without the written permission of the publisher except in the case of brief quotations embodied in critical articles and reviews.

Unless otherwise indicated, all Scripture taken from the New King James Version. Copyright © 1982 by Thomas Nelson, Inc. Used by permission. All rights reserved.

Scripture quotations marked NLT are taken from the Holy Bible, New Living Translation, copyright 1996, 2004. Used by permission of Tyndale House Publishers, Inc., Wheaton, Illinois 60189. All rights reserved.

To the memory of my parents,
Graham C. and Martha West Cochrane

and

former mother-in-law,
Hazel Deaton Leonard;

and for

Stephan, Ashley, Colin, Jacob, Zachary,
Kathy, Stuart and Mary

Trust in the Lord with all your heart,
And lean not on your own understanding;
In all your ways acknowledge Him
And He shall direct your paths.

Proverbs 3:5-6

CONTENTS

FOREWORD

Throughout my life God has signaled His presence and concern for me through a series of remarkable events. Some would call them *coincidences* while others would simply term them *happenstances.* Squire Rushnell, in a series of his books, calls such events "God winks," a term his grandmother taught him. Whatever term one uses, to me each denotes events that occur so improbably that they engender awe and wonder. Recently Sue Goldsmith, a dear new friend from Maryland who entered my life as the result of such an event, suggested I write about these *coincidences* and how they have comforted and reassured me throughout my life during times of change and challenge. This little book is the result of Sue's suggestion. I pray that my experiences provide comfort and reassurance to all who read about them.

The journey I recount in these pages begins when I was seven years old. It is a simple story of loss and centers on the death of my grandfather and shortly thereafter, the disappearance of my beloved collie, Lassie. It describes how God answered a grieving child's three years of prayers in a special and surprising manner.

God's answer to those heartfelt prayers became the foundation of my conviction that God hears and responds to all our prayers no matter how trivial they may seem to others. During the 65 years since Lassie "came home," my journey of faith has led me upon a winding and rocky path that has included periods of profound depression, a series of serious physical illnesses that include polio, ankylosing spondylitis, multiple sclerosis, post-polio syndrome and a miraculous rescue from a horrific house fire. However, the pain from these challenges did not equal the pain I experienced from the breakup of my family and the medically-necessitated geographical relocation that led to a lengthy separation from my three children.

For nearly 50 years God's coincidences have provided the certain knowledge that He is by my side. Both his Word and His "winks'" have provided ". . . a lamp to my feet and a light to my path." Psalm 119:105

As you share my journey you will discover how God's coincidences have guided me through the transformative trials and turbulence of my life. Through the reassurance and strength these occurrences have provided, God has led me to be of service to others in ways I could never have envisioned. Sharing my story with you is part of the process by which God continues to transform my past pain into the joy I experience each day.

I pray my story will bless you just as it has blessed me so that you may become more aware of the similarly coincidental yet significant events that occur in your own life. Through them you will experience God's affirming and guiding presence.

Lynn Cochrane Leonard
Lookout Mountain
Phoenix, Arizona
May 11, 2010

CHAPTER ONE: LASSIE COME HOME

Greenville, South Carolina: 1946-1951

As I look back over the 72 years of life God has so graciously granted me I am awed by His faithfulness, His tenderness and His generosity. And as I consider where to begin the story of His guidance in my life, I turn to my earliest awareness of the many coincidences by which God has signaled His presence to me.

My parents came of age when the Great Depression was gripping our nation by the throat. Each of them felt blessed to be employed. Each was even more blessed to have been raised in Christian homes. Dad was a Methodist as was his mother, and Mother was a Southern Baptist as were her parents. When my parents married in April 1937 they planned to postpone starting a family because Mother earned considerably more than Dad. However, Dad who was a second son, was eager to produce his parents' first grandchild and I arrived two weeks shy of their ten month anniversary. Due to a clotting disorder that threatened my life, my parents incurred large medical bills that continued accumulating throughout my first year of life.

My health was not the only challenge confronting my parents. Shortly after my birth Mother's mother was diagnosed with terminal breast cancer. My maternal grandmother died in late November 1941. Seven days later the Japanese bombed Pearl Harbor and this drew America into World War II. Mother had re-entered the work force and was on duty in Army Intelligence at the Greenville Army Air Base in Greenville, South Carolina as the bombs rained down on Hawaii. Mother's father whom I called "Poppa West" moved from Greenville to Charlotte, North Carolina, to New York City, then returned to Charlotte and eventually to Greenville as the General Freight Agent for the Piedmont and Northern Railway during the war years. It was wonderful to have Poppa West back home in Greenville where I could see him at least once or twice a week whether at the Poinsett Hotel where he lived or at the house where my mother had grown up and which her mother had left to me before her death. By the summer of 1945 Mother had recovered from the loss of her mother and was overjoyed to have her father nearby.

August 14, 1945. Our gang of 10 boys and me marched joyfully around the neighborhood beating on pots, pans and garbage can lids as we celebrated VJ Day and the end of World War II. I had been one of the fortunate children whose fathers were not in service. My dad had been 4-F due to his extremely elevated blood pressure but in April 1945 the Draft Board had summoned him to Fort Jackson for a pre-induction physical. They checked Dad's blood pressure over several days. On the third day, they checked his blood pressure reading before he even got out of bed. "Normal enough. Go home. You have six weeks to arrange your affairs. Your Draft Board will notify you of your reclassification and when and where to report for duty."

However, several world-altering events intervened in rapid succession. President Roosevelt died on April 12, 1945, the very day on which Dad was told he would be inducted. Then Adolph Hitler committed suicide on April 30 and Germany surrendered unconditionally on May 8, 1945, marking the end of World War II in Europe. When V-J Day was declared in August after the bombing of Hiroshima on August 6 and Nagasaki on August 9, Dad still had not been told to report for active duty.

On that glorious day, August 14, 1945, Dad was in a jubilant mood as was everyone else in our nation and most people throughout the world. I believe it was mid-afternoon. I was tending our Victory garden in the back yard when I heard Dad calling, "*Carolyn, come see what I have." I was surprised to hear his voice at that time of day. As I drew near where Dad was standing by the back porch steps, I saw he was cradling something in his arms. Dad was smiling broadly and it had been such a long time since he had looked so happy and relaxed. His arms held a beautiful ball of tawny and white fluff which turned out to be an eight week old purebred Collie puppy. Mother, Dad and I had seen the movie *Lassie Come Home* in downtown Greenville a few years earlier and ever afterwards I had begged for a collie of my own. And now here was my own Lassie, a gift from my parents to me in celebration of the war's end. It was the very best day of my young life.

Lassie and I were inseparable in an era without leash laws. Lassie escorted me to school and back home again, just as in the movie Lassie escorted Roddy McDowall's character to and from his school in Scotland. My Lassie played chase with all of us in the neighborhood or would sit attentively while watching us play softball, football or tag. She might disappear for a few hours but Lassie never missed her dinner. She never disappeared for days at a time as did my cat, Inky. Once Inky disappeared for nearly two weeks but during a Greenville deluge we heard meowing at the back door. There was Inky with four gray and white tiger-striped kittens, tiny replicas of the tomcat Inky hated. Dad told me Inky had been too embarrassed to give birth at home as was her custom.

"It took an act of God—this downpour of Biblical proportions—before Inky was willing to present proof that old, gray tiger tomcat had gotten her in the family way!"

Inky and Lassie were great friends. Dad was an amateur photographer and took several pictures that are my favorites to this day. Lassie had just been bathed and dried. She is lying on her side in the green grass and Inky is curled atop Lassie. Dad's camera captured an image of a solid shiny mass of black fur amidst the lustrous, tawny brown of Lassie's coat.

With the end of World War II and the presence of both Poppa West and Lassie in my life I had never been happier. My parents

---

*   I did not change my name to "Lynn" until 1954.

had a turbulent marriage. Since I was an only child, their angry words and constant fighting were painful for me to endure. Lassie and Poppa West provided the nurturing and comfort my parents were often too self involved to offer me. I was bereft when Poppa West died suddenly three days after Christmas in 1946. My parents did not allow me to attend his funeral nor to go with them down state to Camden, South Carolina where they buried him next to my grandmother in the historic Quaker Cemetery. Nor was I allowed to express sadness. This was the era when children were to "speak only when spoken to."

Yet Lassie listened to me while I poured out my grief. She never chastised me and was a source of constant support.

LASSIE AT HOME

1946: Lassie with unknown feline companion, the author and her mother, Martha West Cochrane

However, I soon discovered, nature's rules apply equally to dogs as well as to cats who roam at will. Dogs also soon present their owners with unplanned bonuses or burdens—depending on their owners' points of view. When my parents told me Lassie would be having puppies they made it clear we would be selling all of them or giving them away. In due time a neighbor called early one morning to say Lassie had given birth across the street in his side yard. Dad let me help bring Lassie and her brood of ten puppies home to our back porch where we left the door open so she could go in and out at will. We made a bed for Lassie and her large family from old bedspreads and she seemed quite contented as she nursed and licked each puppy in turn.

My parents and I watched the puppies grow. Their different personalities appeared early. Three of the males were very aggressive and were much larger than the rest of their siblings. I often helped the littlest guy get up to a "lunch counter" early so there would be enough milk for him. They began opening their eyes on the eighth day. Dad said this meant they were all quite "precocious," one of Dad's favorite words. All went well for ten days and then disaster struck.

Lassie had a new habit of excusing herself from her maternal duties for a somewhat longer period of time. Dad explained, "Like all mothers, she needs to take a brief break from her maternal duties. You could keep her puppies company until she returns."

And so it became my custom to stand watch over the puppies during Lassie's absence. For some reason I do not recall, on this particular early afternoon of the puppies' tenth day of life I was sitting on our front steps and putting on my roller skates. I was aware that Lassie was standing curbside while waiting for Mills Avenue traffic to clear. I had glanced down to tighten the wheels on my skates when I heard the screeching of tires. I looked up just in time to see Lassie sail up and over the cab of a 16-wheel semi that was headed south on Mills Avenue and to see her land in the path of a northbound sedan. Lassie's pitiful yelping quickly followed the loud and sickening sounds that preceded them. Across the whole width of Mills Avenue's I could see Lassie lying inert about ten feet ahead of the tan sedan that had come to a complete stop. Before I could reach Lassie and the man driving the sedan I saw Lassie rise to her feet. Then before the driver could stop her from moving, Lassie ran back to my side of the street and made a beeline to the house next door where she hid under their side porch next to our driveway.

Fortunately Mother was home. When she heard those two horrendous thuds and Lassie's frantic yelping she ran to the front yard where she joined me in trying to lure Lassie to come to us. When I attempted to crawl under the porch next door in an effort to reach Lassie, she snarled and snapped at me. Mother went inside and called the veterinarian who came immediately. He sedated Lassie and took her with him back to his animal hospital. Dad was out of town and when the vet phoned with the news that Lassie could be saved only if we consented to having her left front leg amputated at the shoulder, Mother placed a call to Dad. My parents knew how much I love Lassie and they authorized the vet to do everything possible to save her.

Mother took me to visit Lassie several times each week. Between visits we were busy feeding Lassie's ten puppies. At first we fed them using eye droppers, then turkey basters. After a week or so we began placing milk in five pie tins which we then set atop our picnic table. At first the puppies stepped in the tins and didn't know how to lap the milk. It required lots of patience to lift them out of the pie tins and to replace what they overturned only to repeat the entire process again. When Lassie's pups were six weeks old we began advertising their availability. Within two weeks all puppies had been adopted and we settled down to await Lassie's return.

When Lassie came home from the hospital she was an entirely different dog. She snarled at anyone who came near her, even me. The vet explained this was likely due to her major head injury. My parents gave in to my pleas that we give Lassie time to adjust to us again. However, by early August they persuaded me that the sound of traffic near our house was too upsetting to Lassie and that she would be far happier somewhere in the country. The man who brought our eggs and butter was eager to give Lassie a home. He had a three-legged German Shepherd and thought the two dogs would make great companions.

It was a very sad day when I told Lassie "goodbye." I could barely watch as she rode away with her new owner. My only comfort was that every two weeks when we received our eggs and country butter I would learn how Lassie was faring with her new family and her three-legged canine companion.

The next two weeks passed slowly but finally Saturday morning arrived and there was Mr. Bigelow's familiar sedan. I ran to the greet him as he came up the walkway but he was not smiling. I knew something was terribly wrong.

"Missy, I'm so sorry. But Lassie jumped out of the car and ran away before I had a chance to grab her leash. We've searched everywhere for her and posted signs in town and all over the countryside but no one's seen hide nor hair of a three-legged collie. All I can say is I'll keep trying and I'll let y'all know as soon as we get word of her whereabouts."

The grieving I'd been doing for Lassie ever since her accident now deepened. I began to ask anyone I met if they had seen a three-legged collie dog. With hindsight I recognize that the earlier loss of my grandfather intensified my grief over Lassie's disappearance. Decades later my father told me he had been asked to meet with my grammar school principal and second grade teacher, both of whom thought I needed special attention because I was no longer the happy, outgoing little girl they had known before. They told Dad that all I talked about was finding Lassie. For the next three years each night I prayed that Lassie would be found and for three years. Whenever I met a stranger for the first time, I asked if they had seen or heard of a three-legged collie dog.

The summer of 1949 I attended Girl Scout Camp WaBak for a second summer. I adored the camp routine and being with so many girls my age. As an only child I had often been lonely. That was one reason Lassie had meant so much to me. She was always there and happy to be with me just as I was happy to be with her. Sunday at Camp WaBak was Parents Day when parents came to visit their children. This particular Parents Day was like all the rest and my routine did not vary. I made the rounds of visiting parents, asking the same question I'd been asking for nearly three years.

"Have you seen or heard of a three-legged collie dog who took up in your area about three years ago?"

By now I anticipated a negative response such as, "No missy. Can't say that I have. Did you lose your dog?" I would then give my name and who my parents were and that we lived in Greenville and then I would approach some other visiting parents. One of my favorite campers was from Taylors, South Carolina. Her parents lived on a farm out from town and I approached them with my usual question. This time I received an entirely different response from LuBelle's father.

"Why yes! I *have* heard of a three-legged collie dog. A dog like that took up with the butcher's family near 'bout three years ago. Looked like she'd received an injury to her head. She hates cars and trucks and they have to keep her tied up on their property or she'll chase after any vehicle like she thinks it's some sort of demon."

My parents were not visiting me that particular Parents Day but I wrote them about what I'd learned. The following Sunday we made the trip to Taylors. In town obtained directions to the butcher's farm. As we entered the deeply rutted driveway we saw a hand-lettered sign posted high on the trunk of a chinaberry tree: BEWARE OF DOG. We heard Lassie's fierce barking before we saw her charge towards us from around the corner of the house. We also heard a woman shout,

"Ya'll wait till I get this here dog tied up. She don't like strangers." But I was already out of the car. Kneeling beside our Packard I patted my thigh and called "Come Lassie, come here." Lassie came straight to me and licked away my tears."

At some point I noticed a boy in a wheelchair sitting on the porch. He looked to be about my age. He had been calling "Shep, come here!" at the top of his lungs at the same time I was calling for Lassie to come to me. Suddenly there was silence as everyone watched Lassie and me.

"Why I never!" exclaimed the mother. "Shep done never take to anyone like she be taking to your little girl." My parents then explained who we were and told Lassie's story. As I listened and petted Lassie I was glancing up at the boy in the wheelchair. Even from a distance I could tell he understood Lassie had been my dog long before she became his. I also realized he was probably a victim of polio. Polio had been the scourge of South Carolina the past two summers and parents had kept their children away from swimming pools and movie theaters.

My parents and I heard how "Shep" had just showed up one stormy night. She had hung around and appeared to be half starved and so they fed her and made her a bed in their barn.

"She's been such a blessing for our boy. They have lots in common, you see. Her with her injury and him with his infantile paralysis. She snarls at almost everyone else but she's never snarled at Jimmy. She's just about his only friend. Them other boys don't come 'round no more now that our Jimmy cain't run and play with 'em," his mother explained.

In my heart I knew I could not take Lassie home with us. She'd be totally miserable from all the heavy traffic now thundering up and down Mills Avenue since the city had made it a truck route. Lassie had spent nearly three years with this family and she was this crippled boy's major source of comfort. I knew I had to leave Lassie in that peaceful setting with the family that had rescued her and given her a good home.

God had heard my prayers, prayers that had persisted for three years. In Sunday School and church I had learned we should "pray without ceasing" and give thanks in all circumstances. Even though during those three years my parents had tried to instruct me that sometimes God answered our prayers with a firm "No," I could not believe I would never learn what had become of Lassie. Through all those years I was confident God would provide an answer.

That Lassie was found as an answer to my persistent prayers has provided courage and comfort throughout my life. It became the first in a series of events that together formed a chain, each event providing a coincidental yet necessary link to finding Lassie. While many educated people who sincerely believe in a Creator God do not believe He plays an active role in our daily lives, I strongly disagree. Had I not been attending Camp WaBak that summer I would not have found Lassie. I was at Camp WaBak because I sold more Girl Scout calendars than any other girl in South Carolina. As I sold those calendars at church, on the streets of downtown Greenville and door-to-door in many neighborhoods, I had posed my poignant question concerning Lassie. Thinking back upon those days, it is possible that many who purchased calendars from me did so because of my story about Lassie. That is something I can never know for certain.

Here is what I do know. Had I not won the Girl Scout calendar sales contest I would not have been at Camp WaBak. I would not have met LuBelle and her parents from whom I learned that a three-legged collie dog came to Taylors—a tiny town some 30 miles distant from where Lassie escaped from Mr. Bigelow—and was living there with the town butcher and his family. I had been grateful to leave Lassie with her new owner. He was a polio victim and could not walk while I could run and play at will.

It is indeed ironic that later that same summer while attending Camp WaBak I, too, contracted polio. And while in my case polio did considerable damage that years later did require extensive surgery to my spine, it did not limit the use of my legs and confine me to a wheelchair as was the case for Lassie's new master. When I returned to Greenville in 1954, I learned that despite her massive injuries, Lassie lived a very long life and provided many years of joy to the boy who became her master. Lassie had indeed come home.

> **Ask, and it will be given to you;
> seek, and you will find; knock, and
> it will be opened to you. For everyone
> who asks receives; and he who
> seeks finds; and to him who knocks
> it will be opened.**
>
> **Matthew 7:7-8**

CHAPTER TWO: "I'LL WALK WITH GOD"
Greensboro, North Carolina: 1954-1955

While serving as a junior counselor at Camp WaBak in the summer of 1953 I was deeply disappointed when my parents arrived unexpectedly to insist I leave camp immediately and come home with them. Dad had a new position with the Federal Home Loan Bank in Greensboro, North Carolina and there was much to do before moving day. My parents were determined I begin school in Greensboro on time in late August. No teenager enjoys being uprooted. I had a steady boyfriend, a great guy named Bobby. We had recently patched things up following a month-long break up. Bobby and I had weathered multiple challenges together. He had been amazingly supportive during my hospitalization for a ruptured appendix and again that same year during the six weeks I was confined to bed with severe back pain. We vowed to remain true to one another and still planned to marry after graduating from college. Ours was an eight year plan and we had already weathered nearly two years of it.

Greensboro was a lovely town and Greensboro Senior High was a welcoming place. When Miss Abernathy, who lived next door, discovered I had edited my junior high school paper she welcomed me on staff with the weekly school newspaper, the Greensboro Senior High School *High Life*. At Greensboro High scholastic achievement was no barrier to acceptance. In Greensboro I found it much easier to fit in with a group of girls who could not have been more welcoming and more academically oriented. For the first time I felt totally at ease at school. In Greensboro from the outset I introduced myself as Lynn Cochrane.

When I recall my high school days they were truly the proverbial best of times and worst of times. The mid-1950s era was one of classical style and exhilarating romance. There was no generational divide regarding music and there was music for every taste. The range was amazing. Parents as well as teenagers thrilled to Mario Lanza's glorious voice when he sang "Be My Love" and "Because of You." Then there was Elvis who was just then releasing "Love Me Tender" and "Jail House Rock." Patsy Cline's "Crazy" and "I Fall to Pieces" were Country music hits along with Homer and Jethro's "Jambalaya." Judy Garland, Doris Day, Ella Fitzgerald and Billie Holiday were popular female vocalists together with Rosemary Clooney, Jo Stafford, Bing Crosby, Perry Como, Pat Boone, Tennessee Ernie Ford, Johnny Cash and Bobby Darin were popular male vocalists of that musically rich and diverse era.

Style mattered in all things whether fashion, furniture or automobiles. Ford and GM offered the small T-Bird and Corvette, respectively, and Studebaker introduced the Hawk. Movies such *The High and The Mighty, Giant, Rebel Without A Cause, Rear Window, High Society, High Noon* and *Love Is A Many-Splendored Thing* appealed to both males and females. Movies employed compelling plots and music utilized intricate melody and harmonics. High school prom nights in the Fabulous Fifties did not involve limousines and rented hotel rooms for after-prom celebrations. Post-prom entertainment occurred in private homes. I vividly recall Prom Night 1954 in Greensboro. Many of the young men wore white dinner jackets, plaid Bermuda shorts, red cummerbunds and bowties and red knee socks. All the girls wore pastel gowns of tulle with billowing skirts supported by hoops or stiff crinolines. We slow danced to " Ebb Tide," and "Too Young" or jitterbugged to "Rock Around the Clock."

As my sophomore year came to an end I became assistant editor of the *High Life*. The staff had enjoyed a wonderfully exciting trip to New York City where our school paper brought home several top journalism awards. Becoming assistant editor in my junior year meant I would likely serve as editor-in-chief during my senior year. In addition, I would write a daily column for the *Greensboro Record* which meant that for the first time I would be earning money as a journalist. Life was wonderful. The only dark clouds on my horizon were my difficulty with algebra and geometry and my long distance romance with Bobby. While I had attended the various proms throughout the year with several different escorts, I was not dating anyone on a routine basis.

Over the Fourth of July holiday following that glorious May prom night I met Steve Leonard, my amazingly handsome and talented husband-to-be. I had just returned home from a visit with Bobby and it had not gone well. Steve was scheduled to enter the Army that September and his friend, Cordelia, told me, "Lynn, you're about to miss your chance to meet a really terrific guy!"

Two days after Steve and I met, Mother and I went to Ocean Drive Beach, South Carolina. Mother allowed me to invite Steve to join us there for the weekend. Steve and I strolled the strand both by sun and by moonlight and we rode the rollercoaster at neighboring Myrtle Beach. Back in Greensboro we went to many movies, most memorably *The High and The Mighty*. Its theme song by the same name became "our song." In early September before Steve left on the bus to Fort Jackson, South Carolina for basic training we became engaged. I was inordinately proud of my engagement ring and also proud that I was the assistant editor of *High Life*. Life was coming my way. My parents had reconciled after a six month separation and they had finally found a point of agreement. Both thought Steve was an exceptional young man.

Then on Tuesday, November 30, I found myself in Moses Cone Hospital as the result of a fall down the stairs at school. Sixteen days later I underwent extensive back surgery to stabilize my spine which was rotating drastically due to an atrophied back muscle resulting from the polio I contracted when I was 11. What previously had been considered a rather benign case of polio now appeared to have produced more damaging effects. Having completed basic training,

Steve arrived home on extended leave the day before my surgery on December 16. Whenever pain roused me from the narcotic haze my doctors kept me in, Steve was there, holding my hand and smiling encouragement. However, I had overheard the orthopedist and neurosurgeon tell my parents I likely would never walk again. During surgery they encountered a vast amount of damage to spinal nerves that were embedded in scar tissue.

The prospect of Steve tied to a paraplegic in a wheelchair overwhelmed me. On Steve's last day with me before he left for Fort Jackson I returned his ring. A week later his Aunt Enid and Uncle Wilber visited from High Point on my 17th birthday. Enid tearfully begged me to accept Steve's ring again. As much as I wanted to do so, I could not allow Steve to tie himself and his future to a cripple.

I spent a total of ten weeks lying flat on my back, encased in a body cast that extended from my collar bone to my groin. I was not allowed to have even a small pillow beneath my head or to raise my head at all. Friends from school came often and I tried to study. Prism glasses enabled me to read books that were open and placed flat on my chest. I remained on heavy doses of Demerol and through both sleep and music I tried to escape the intense fear and helplessness I felt as I thought about my future in a wheelchair. I could not believe that would be the future God had in store for me.

Mother had given me a Webcor hi-fi for Christmas and I repeatedly listened to Mario Lanza sing "I'll Walk with God" from the movie, *The Student Prince*. As I listened I recalled how much I had loved running cross country all over the hilly streets of my former hometown in Greenville. As I lay in bed—when I wasn't imagining running—I recalled the long hikes I had taken as a camper at WaBak and all the miles I had walked on the beach at Ocean Drive during my many summer vacations there. Between Christmas 1954 and Valentine's Day 1955 in my imagination I walked and ran countless miles each day.

My imagination helped me in other ways. I taught myself to deal with my back pain by mentally transferring my torso—the part of me covered by the body cast—to the empty bed in my hospital room. When Dr. Register, my orthopedist, asked how I was managing with so little Demerol, my explanation was matter-of-fact.

"I just take the part of me that's in the cast and put it in the bed over there. That puts some distance between me and the pain." Evidently this explanation alarmed Dr. Register. Within hours a new doctor visited me. Dr. G. was a psychiatrist and after examining me, he pronounced me sane. However, when he met with my parents and me the next day his assessment surprised me.

"Your daughter is a brilliant young woman who can go one of two ways. Her future can either be extremely bright wherein she will make a valuable contribution to society or alternatively, she could wind up an eccentric in Greenwich Village. I have absolutely no idea which path she will take."

Following my surgery Dr. Register had promised I would be allowed up and out of bed in 60 days. Finally on Valentine's Day two solemn nurses entered my room and announced they were there to help me try to stand for the first time since I entered the hospital 75 days earlier. I had assumed Dr. Register would remove the body cast prior to allowing me out of bed. Instead, these nurses indicated the time to test my back and legs was now.

"Lynn, we'll support you while you attempt to bear weight and then we will put you right back in bed."

It was obvious to me these nurses were not expecting me to be able to stand on my own. Each supported me under an arm and both of them appeared startled when I insisted they stand back. Instead of falling as they had anticipated, I was able to walk across my room, then across the wide hall, and across the large four-bed ward opposite my room. That night I welcomed Demerol because my long-unused muscles were protesting loudly. Two days later I left the hospital by ambulance. However, I remained in the body cast until Good Friday.

At home in mid-February I had begun the arduous task of working with a homebound teacher to make up all the coursework I had missed in French, American History, Geometry, English, and Biology. First I needed to take make-up final exams in each of these subjects covering the semester that ended in January. Then I needed to cover all of the materials in the second semester for each of these topics. My goal was to take the final exams for this second semester of my junior year together with all my fellow classmates in late May. With considerable effort on my part and superb tutoring by two amazing teachers I passed the fall semester exams.

While it is true I cannot recount any stunning coincidence for this chapter of my life in which I was able to walk despite two surgeons' opinions that I would live the remainder of my life confined to a wheelchair, I do know that it was God who enabled me to walk. I believe it was the Holy Spirit who guided me to engage in several practices that only in recent decades—long after I was guided to use them—are now known to have powerful and positive physical effects.

The combination of music, prayer and what later became known as "visualization" is what I believe repaired spinal nerves that were embedded in scar tissue and had then fragmented when the neurosurgeon attempted to free them. Today we are learning far more about the healing impact of music on the brain and the spirit. Many stroke patients who cannot speak, can in fact, sing. As I lay in my body cast, I imagined myself running and walking as I had done as a child and I did so day in and day out as I listened repeatedly to the following hymn that Mario Lanza sang in The Student Prince.

Only in the latter part of the 20th Century and the first decade of the 21st Century are scientists beginning to plumb the mysteries of how marvelously and with what intricate care our Lord fashioned the connections between our mind, our body and our spirit. Here is but one verse of the song I listened to for hours each day as I prayed to walk again while remembering how it felt to walk and run prior to polio and the fall on the stairs at school.

I'll Walk with God
I'll walk with God from this day on
His helping hand I'll lean upon
This is my prayer, my humble plea,
May the Lord be ever with me.

Lyrics: Paul Francis Webster.
Music: Nicholas Brodszky.

Chapter Three: "Going to the Chapel"
Fort Jackson, SC - Fort Sill, OK: 1955-1956

H owever, a life-changing event occurred prior to taking my final exams. Steve and I decided to marry before he shipped out to Fort Sill in Oklahoma. We were in love and yet financial concerns prompted our shift in plans. We planned for me to remain at my parents' home in Greensboro where I could bank most of the allotment the Army would send me as an Army wife. This plan would provide a fair amount of savings with which to move to California where Steve had already been accepted at the prestigious Los Angeles Art Center for study in Industrial Design. Steve and I were married on May 11, 1955 in a chapel at Fort Jackson, South Carolina. All four parents attended the ceremony even though initially both fathers had been strongly opposed as had Steve's mother. Dad had objected strenuously in a long distance phone call from Vero Beach, Florida where he was working at that time.

Steve had arrived the Friday before Mother's Day for his final leave before shipping out to Fort Sill in Oklahoma. Then during Mother's Day Sunday dinner at the Morning Glory Cafe—Thomasville's only "fine dining" venue—together with Steve's mother, Hazel, and my mother, Steve and I gave a most unwelcomed present to Hazel on her special day. My mother already knew and was supportive of our wedding plans as were Steve's Aunt Enid and Uncle Wilbur. But

Steve' father, Paul, had protested our plans even more forcefully than had my father. When Steve left his Thomasville home late that Sunday afternoon with my mother and me (we would take Steve to the train depot to join his company at Fort Jackson prior to his departure on Thursday for Fort Sill, Oklahoma), Paul angrily declared he would not serve as best man because he strongly believed Steve was making the biggest mistake of his young life—one he predicted Steve would live to regret.

"Son, you are way too young to settle down with any gal—much less almost the first one you've ever dated and one whose health isn't at all good!"

However, Paul did change his mind about attending the wedding and even stood up as best man for his only son. Many years later I learned that while waiting in the chapel's vestibule and listening for the organ's cue to enter the sanctuary, Paul had whispered to Steve, "It's not too late to change your mind. You can duck out that door behind us!"

When Steve later told me about this conversation, I laughed. While awaiting the same musical cue to proceed down the aisle on my father's arm, Dad had looked me square in the eye and proclaimed, "Carolyn, you don't have to go through with this. We can just walk away with no real harm done."

Steve and I had one night together before he boarded the train to Fort Sill and I returned home to Greensboro to continue studying to take the final exams that would conclude my eventful junior year in high school. But two more major interruptions occurred. Dad flew back home from Vero Beach and entered Moses Cone Hospital with severe stomach pain from which he frequently suffered as the result of ulcers that plagued him and which his internists could never detect on film. Then the day following Dad's admission to the same hospital where I had spent three months earlier in the year, Mother was admitted there for surgery to remove a goose egg-sized breast lump that had not been evident six weeks earlier during her annual physical. The following day Mother underwent a radical mastectomy and spent the next month in the hospital. Dad left the hospital against medical advice and returned to Florida to pick up his car and conclude his work there.

Prior to his departure Dad told me, "Carolyn, you are married and your place is with Steve. You made this adult decision without consulting me or seeking my blessing. The two of you have to learn that adult decisions mean assuming adult responsibilities. Your place is with your husband." After Mother came home from the hospital and Dad returned from Florida, I left in early July to join Steve in Oklahoma. We had first met only 12 months earlier.

❧

Seated next to the window I could see the wing and two engines of the DC-7 as we flew from Greensboro to Atlanta on the morning of July 9. Gazing at the clouds I mentally reviewed all the multiple challenges Steve and I had surmounted in the 12 months since we met. These major milestones had occurred with dizzying rapidity. Steve had transitioned from civilian to military life; I had endured spinal surgery and the prognosis I would never walk again which led me to return Steve's ring. Then came our whirlwind wedding with only a 12 hour honeymoon followed rapidly by my parents hospitalizations and Mother's cancer diagnosis and subsequent surgery.

My lifelong fear of flying began during the second leg of my flight to Lawton, Oklahoma. Some 30 minutes after leaving Atlanta my seat companion alerted me to the fact that one of the two engines on the left wing was on fire. The pilot's calm voice announcing our return to Atlanta did nothing to allay my anxiety. When I missed the plane in Dallas that would have taken me on to Lawton, I collapsed in tears as I watched the plane take off and heard the ticket agent inform me the next flight to Lawton would be the following day. He then cheerfully explained I could hop on a bus due to leave in 15 minutes if I didn't want to wait in Dallas for the next day's flight.

I had neither phone number nor street address for the apartment Steve had rented in Lawton. Nor could I remember the name of Steve's unit at Fort Sill and his letters to me were in my luggage which was on some plane somewhere. In desperation I asked the long distance operator to connect me to anyone at Fort Sill. When a private answered the phone, I barely had time to blurt out my situation before I was told my bus was about to leave. After collapsing in my seat I learned the bus was heading to Wichita Falls. While geography was not my strong suit, I remembered that Wichita was in Kansas and that Kansas was north of Oklahoma. Exhausted and totally discouraged, I cried myself to sleep. My next awareness came when the bus driver shook my shoulder. "Wakeup, Miss. This is the end of the line. You have to get off here." Opening my eyes I discovered I was the only passenger still on board.

Half awake and assuming that like Dorothy in the Wizard of Oz I would find myself in Kansas, I exited the bus and was overjoyed to find Steve standing—hands on his hips—and looking more serious than I had ever seen him look before. No sight was ever more welcomed than was his handsome young face at that moment. In wonderment I asked Steve how he had known I would arrive in Lawton by bus.

Steve grinned. "Well, it was a total fluke! When you weren't on the plane I placed a long distance call to the Dallas Airport and explained to the operator I needed to be connected to someone there who could trace my wife who had not arrived in Lawton from Dallas as scheduled. That operator said, " 'Sir, your wife missed her connecting flight in Dallas and she will be arriving by bus later this evening. You might check with the Bus Station to see when the bus from Dallas is due to arrive. There's one scheduled stop in Wichita Falls, Texas.' "

Steve had not received the message I'd left for him at Fort Sill. Instead, he experienced the miracle of connecting with the same telephone operator who had placed my call to him at Fort Sill. This operator evidently had remained on the line for both calls long enough to realize she had the information Steve needed in order to find his missing bride!

Beginning in July 1955 we struggled valiantly to exist on the $178.30 the Army paid a married Private E2 each month. At each month's end we were always drastically short of cash. I remember collecting discarded pop bottles along the road to turn into the grocery store for a nickel each. I also recall the Sunday dinner Steve and I shared that consisted of one can of black eyed peas. Letters from Steve's mother were always welcomed because they invariably contained a few dollars with which we could purchase something to help us stave off starvation.

Our dire straits resulted in part from a disastrous financial decision we had made when the clutch on the 1947 Ford we owned debt-free needed to be replaced. A new clutch cost $29 which we didn't have. That is when we fell into the clutches of Mad Man Madden, one of Lawton's most aggressive used car dealers. We used our 1947 Ford as down payment for a 1951 Pontiac. No cash was needed so we had a car that was immediately drivable. But we also took on a monthly car payment of $43.10. Our rent was $48 and this left but 20 cents of my monthly allotment check of $91.30. All that remained was the $87 Steve received in cash each month. Those dollars had to cover the cost of gas, food and utilities and laundering Steve's fatigues. (My attempt to starch and iron his fatigues was spectacularly unsuccessful.) We were unable to save anything for Steve's education. Many months we ran out of money before pay day. When pay day rolled around each month we would treat ourselves to a pizza at Bianco's Italian Restaurant. Nothing before or since has ever tasted as delicious as those pizzas!

In December we made a flying trip back to North Carolina in our 1951 Pontiac. We planned to divide our time between my parents' home in Greensboro and Steve's parents' home 30 miles away in Thomasville. We stopped in Thomasville first where all four of our parents had been awaiting our arrival, their anxiety heightened by concerns that our 1947 Ford was less than roadworthy. They were both stunned and disappointed when we arrived in our "new" Pontiac. Our parents had collaborated to purchase a newer Ford for us to drive back to Oklahoma. Their disappointed did not come close to matching our own. All Steve and I could think about was the $43.10 monthly car payment. Before we left to spend Christmas Eve with my parents and to return the following day for Christmas dinner with Steve, his parents and sisters, his father presented us with an early Christmas present, a matching pair of red pajamas.

SANTA'S HELPERS

*Christmas 1955. Lynn and Steve in matching Santa-
red pajamas, Christmas gifts from Steve's dad for
our first Christmas as a married couple.*

At Easter we camped out overnight with our friends Lilly and
George Marcotte on Wichita Mountain about 25 miles northwest
of Lawton. The amphitheater there is the setting for the nation's
longest-running Easter Passion Play, *The Prince of Peace.* The Chapel
of the Holy City, built of native granite, was constructed with Federal
money by the WPA and completed in 1936. The design, inspired by
a church in Alexandria, Virginia, is reminiscent of an Old World
Temple. In the interior of the Chapel are wood carvings, paintings
and murals of the Biblical days of Christ.

Government land in the Wichita National Forest Reserve was
designated by the U.S. Government for the site of the Holy City
and its Easter Pageant. The nationally famous Easter Pageant is a
dramatization of the life of Christ and is held on Easter Eve. Today
I give thanks there was a time when Federal money was used to
provide employment during the Great Depression for men to build
projects, even those of a religious nature.

Following a long night outdoors among the granite boulders,
in the chilly dawn we watched the Easter sunrise in a setting we
imagined closely resembled the Holy Land. It was during that pageant

I was first moved by the austere beauty of the buttes surrounding us. I had no way of knowing then that seven years later I would make my home in the valley of the Sonora desert surrounded by similar buttes.

Here I have lived for more than 46 years, often recalling this verse from one of my favorite hymns.

> *Beneath the cross of Jesus I fain would take my stand,*
> *The shadow of a mighty rock within a weary land;*
> *A home within the wilderness, a rest upon the way,*
> *From the burning of the noontide heat, and the*
> *burden of the day.*

Elizabeth Clephane 1872

I wrote the following poem 34 years after Steve and I camped out in Oklahoma while attending the Prince of Peace pageant.

Desert Manna

Who thrives in April's desert climes
Yet withered where wisteria wept?
This broken daughter of the storied South
Whom You banished to these barren buttes.
Here Your sun's fierce cauterie—
Searing hotter than self-hate—
Burnished me beneath
An inverted azure bowl,
Then cleansed me with elemental force.

Your desert did not deign to tremble
Beneath my futile, stamping feet.
No boulders budged; no mountains
Echoed my mewling rage.
In simple, sizzling silence
You declared Yourself.

You set me down beside saguaro sentinels,
Cosseted me with cholla,
Then bade me rest
Within a nest of prickly pear.
"Fear not!" Your whisper commanded.
"Others have sought solace here,
Have winnowed wisdom in this desert crib.
Rest here and heed my voice where
Coyotes call and eagles soar."

Beneath the spines that pierced
My seeking palms Your cactus
Proffered sustenance.
Among Your thorns at last held fast
I am still and know Your love.

Easter 1990
Lookout Mountain
Phoenix, Arizona

Chapter Four: Needle in a Haystack

North Carolina to New York: 1956-1959

Steve received an early discharge from the Army and we left Fort Sill in September 1956. Steve had changed his plan to attend the Art Center in Los Angeles when the four car manufacturers we had queried regarding their recommendations for design schools all responded and listed Pratt Institute as the best place to pursue a Bachelor of Industrial Design degree. Late in August, a letter from Pratt notified Steve of his provisional admission. They specified his admission was based upon the exceptional portfolio he had submitted. They found his high school grades and lack of art classes to be of concern.

With high hopes and light hearts we packed our few possessions in our 1951 Pontiac. We headed home to the Piedmont area of North Carolina where our respective parents awaited us, Steve's parents in Thomasville and mine in Greensboro. However, there was one cloud on our horizon—the possibility that I might be pregnant. Upon our arrival I confided this possibility to my mother who quickly arranged for me to see the family doctor. Back then it was necessary for a rabbit's life to be sacrificed, requiring a wait of several hours for the laboratory findings to reach the doctor.

Steve and I were in Thomasville with his favorite cousin, Sue, in a theater waiting for Grace Kelley's last movie, *The Swan*, to begin. While waiting I used the payphone in the lobby and called home to discover what Mother had learned from the family doctor. I could tell from Mother's excited voice that I needed to brace for news that would totally derail the plans Steve and I had made for our immediate future.

With our plans unraveling even before we left North Carolina and our first child due to arrive in late April, I experienced anxiety as never before. Even if I were able to find a job despite my pregnancy, how long would I be allowed to work? (In the 1950s companies were not obliged to hire a pregnant woman nor did most companies allow her to remain in the workforce throughout her pregnancy. Pregnant women were considered unreliable workers and a potential legal liability.)

We had Steve's Army "mustering out" pay of roughly $700, two suitcases and a pledge from our parents of $75 in combined monthly support. Only two young people endowed with equal shares of optimism and naiveté would have dared such a daunting adventure with such paltry resources.

Steve and I were experiencing a crash course in how life can derail one's plans. As Steve and I traveled by train from Greensboro en route to Grand Central Station in New York, the immortal words of Scotland's beloved poet Robert Burns rang in my ears, rhythmically keeping time to the clickety-clack of the train: "The best laid plans o' mice an' men/ gang aft agley and /lea'e us naught but grief an' pain/ for promised joy." (from "Ode To a Mouse") I had learned these words at my mother's knee. That they were proving all too true was driven home by two additional disappointments.

Steve and I had counted upon three additional sources of income: Steve's GI Bill allotment to cover tuition and provide a monthly check; the salary I planned to earn as a secretary; and Steve's future earnings from Pratt's Work Study Program. Pratt had also included information on its low-cost student housing conveniently located nearby.

We soon learned the only job available to a freshman in the Industrial Design program was a four hour stint in the Pratt library. When Steve mentioned it paid $1.00 an hour I assumed the job was for four hours daily and wondered how we would make ends meet.

Then Steve provided another shocking detail. Due to the rigors of Pratt Institute's freshman Foundation Design course, students in their first year were allowed to work only *four hours each week*. In addition, we had already discovered that the student housing near Pratt was both roach- and rat-ridden with rents that demonstrated the landlords were as relentlessly predatory as were the vermin that occupied their apartments. (I am confident the condition of student housing near Pratt has improved substantially in the intervening 50 years!) The final blow came when we learned it likely would be another two months before Steve's GI Bill allotment began to arrive.

Fortunately Steve's uncle and aunt were housing and feeding us in their Queens apartment during our initial time in New York. After I survived the shock from the deafening noise of my first subway ride, I began a job search that took me to the American Chicle Company in Long Island City. After taking both a typing and steno test as well as an aptitude test, I was congratulated on my performance and hired immediately. When I reported for work on Monday I learned I would train for six months to become the private secretary to the head of the Research and Development Department. Having not disclosed my pregnancy, I quickly realized the ethical and moral dilemmas of allowing myself to undergo a protracted training period when the company was unaware I would be giving birth long before the training was complete. After two weeks I apologetically disclosed my pregnancy to the woman who had hired me. She took pity upon me and transferred me to the large secretarial pool of 60 women where each of us transcribed Dictabelts eight hours daily.

On my third day in the transcription department a scrap of folded typing paper landed on my desk. The woman next to me tapped me on the arm and pointed down the line to my left where another woman was leaning forward and smiling tentatively. She pantomimed I should read the note she had tossed my direction.

Opening the note I read, "Where in the South are you from?"

Hurriedly I scribbled a reply. "South and North Carolina," and sent the note back down the line to the inquirer. Upon the note's return I read the next question.

"Do you know where Thomasville, North Carolina is?"

"Yes. My father and my husband are from Thomasville," I wrote.

"Do you know where Salem Street is in Thomasville?" was the question I next encountered.

I responded, "Yes, my grandmother lives on Salem Street."

The next question left me momentarily stunned. "Do you know a Mrs. G. T. Cochrane?"

My reply left the questioner equally stunned.

"That *is* my grandmother! Why do you ask?"

"My husband is currently auditing the books of Thomasville Furniture Company. Last night he phoned me from Mrs. Cochrane's home where he is renting a room!"

GRANDMOTHER COCHRANE'S HOUSE

301 Salem Street Residence of Mrs. G. T. Cochrane,
Thomasville, North Carolina

Suddenly I felt far less adrift and anonymous as I pondered the odds of arriving in a city of seven million people and finding a job where I sat at a typewriter fewer than six feet away from a woman whose husband had called her the night before from my grandmother's house in a little town of 10,000 souls located more than 470 miles southwest of the American Chicle Company in Queens.

While this amazing coincidence did nothing to ease the financial challenges Steve and I faced over the next few years, I felt immeasurably comforted. God had let me know I was not alone and that He was mindful of me and of our concerns.

❦

Our New York years were an anomalous amalgam of tedium for me, challenge for Steve and exhilaration and exhaustion for us both. Steve paid a heavy price for indulging my aversion to apartments in Brooklyn. His morning commute from Flushing to Pratt involved a three block walk, a 15 minute bus ride to downtown Flushing, taking the IRT subway line and then changing to another subway line that took him into Brooklyn. In late afternoon Steve made the return trip home to Flushing. Commuting gobbled up two and a half hours of his day. Combined with lugging a fishing tackle box of art supplies plus his portfolio of design assignments, Steve's day was both physically and artistically challenging. Back at the apartment Steve then spent another four or five hours on his design course projects. Frequently Steve carted large clay or plaster projects back and forth on the subway as well—projects he had spent hours constructing and which a moment's mishap could totally destroy

Life for me prior to our son Stevie's arrival was more a matter of tedium. When the company paid me a bonus at Christmas and told me I could not return to work again, I was left with four months of long days, no friends and little intellectual stimulation. I wrote poetry, shopped for groceries at least every other day.

At times it was difficult to distract myself from the concern my doctor had stressed regarding Rh incompatibility. I had received a direct transfusion of Rh positive blood from my father when I hemorrhaged at birth due to a clotting disorder and a severe calcium deficiency. Because of that transfusion of Rh positive blood, our first baby was at as much risk of experiencing anemia, jaundice, brain damage or even death as if this were a second pregnancy. My mother's first cousin had lost several babies due to Rh incompatibility.

This was not my only worry. By the middle of April I had gained only ten pounds due to my inability to eat more than a few bites at a time. My diet consisted primarily of peanut butter, grapefruit and milk. I fretted our baby would be underweight and require an incubator. Even my doctor was surprised when Paul Stephan Leonard, Jr. arrived weighing 8 lbs. 10 oz. However, following Stevie's birth, I once again hemorrhaged, but vastly improved treatment and prompt transfusions produced a good result. After five days, Stevie and I were able to go home to our apartment.

Stevie was a robust and good baby and benefited from having both grandmothers visit during his first month on earth as well as the loving attention of his Aunt Jane who spent a month with us. I enjoyed Jane's company and her help with Stevie. Thirteen months later our daughter, Ashley, was born following a challenging pregnancy that confined me to bed for five months. Mother drove from their new home in Little Rock to provide care for me, Stevie and Steve. However, three adults and a toddler in a one bedroom apartment created a tense environment, especially for Steve who had to create design projects while Mother and I watched TV—at a distance of no more than three feet from his drawing board. After Ashley's birth, Dad flew up from Arkansas and helped Mother make the long drive back to Little Rock where they had lived since their arrival on September 4, 1957, the day Governor Faubus called on the National Guard to maintain segregation of the high school.

When Ashley was four months old it became financially necessary for me to work 30 hours each week at night. The reason for our budget shortfall was twofold. Pratt had doubled its tuition and our landlord no longer permitted me to wash diapers on a scrub board in our apartment. While the children and I were absent for a month visiting in North Carolina our neighbors in the building no longer experienced voluminous soapsuds in their sinks and tubs. As a result I had to contract for a diaper service, an item far beyond our ability to purchase. Fortunately my job behind the candy counter at the Roosevelt Theater netted exactly enough to pay for both the diaper service and milk delivered to the door.

Our landlord and landlady were wonderful to us. Jerry White had been an arranger for Jimmy Durante who was his close friend. Mrs. White had been one of the Ziegfeld Follies girls. About 4:00 P.M. each afternoon Mrs. White would play the harp. Throughout the year— except during the winter—my babies and I enjoyed her heavenly music as it wafted through our open bedroom windows.

My weekday afternoon routine was fixed. By 4:00 PM I had the children fed and bathed. By 4:35 I was dressed for work and out the door. Our landlady's sister sat with Stevie and Ashley for the 15 minutes after I left for work and prior to Steve's arrival home at about 4:50 PM. Steve and I met and greeted one another about two blocks from the apartment. At home he would eat the dinner I had prepared for him, get the children to bed no later than 6:30 PM and then work on his design projects. When I arrived home around 11:30 PM Steve was usually still hard at work. It was long after midnight before we bedded down on the new studio couches in our living room since Steve and Ashley now shared our former bedroom.

All was well until late April when I suffered a major depression that placed me in the hospital for a month. My parents insisted that we come to Auburndale, Florida where they had recently relocated. When Steve received financial assistance from the new National Defense Educational Act he was able to return to Pratt for his senior year. Because Thomasville was nearer Pratt than was Auburndale, the children and I relocated to his parents' home in Thomasville while Steve returned to Pratt to finish his degree. He would spend his Christmas break with the children and me and with his parents and his sisters. During his senior year Steve decided to shift his focus from automotive design to furniture design. This shift would place us back in North Carolina—at that time the furniture-producing capital of the United States.

On a glorious June 3, 1960, Steve received his Bachelor of Industrial Design degree from Pratt Institute. His parents and I could not have been more proud. After the four of us returned to North Carolina, Steve secured his first position as a furniture designer in High Point, North Carolina and by mid-July Steve, I and the children once again were able to occupy our own apartment for the first time in more than a year.

Our second son, Colin, was born in February 1962. Once again I experienced a major depressive episode accompanied this time by balance problems. During a brief hospitalization for depression for ten days that included Easter, Steve secured a job as a designer with Drexel Furniture Company in Morganton, North Carolina. He did all the packing for the April move from High Point to Morganton where my parents helped us purchase a new home.

Throughout the summer and fall my depression deepened and my balance problems intensified. It was a tense time for me personally. In fact, my mood mirrored that of the nation following President Kennedy's somber televised address to the nation on October 22, 1962 regarding the Cuban Missile Crisis. It was clear to all who heard President Kennedy's address that the world was poised on the precipice of nuclear war. I followed coverage of the United Nations debate and the Navy blockade. Then my psychiatrist arranged for me to be evaluated in the Neurology Clinic at the University of North Carolina Hospital in Chapel Hill. My doctor had become increasingly concerned about my balance problems, especially after I fell backwards with Colin in my arms.

My October 31 appointment in Chapel Hill came just one week after nuclear war with the USSR was averted when the Russians ships returned home and they agreed to dismantle the missiles in Cuba. While this was a resolution to the nation's missile crisis, it would be many years before I'd learn what the UNC neurologist overlooked in his dismissive evaluation of my inability to stand with my feet together without falling backwards and to the left. In all probability, having been referred by a psychiatrist did not bode well for obtaining an open-minded neurological assessment of my condition. My extensive medical history complete with recent psychiatric hospitalizations likely also diminished this doctor's ability to conduct an appropriate neurological examination. My gender likely was an additional impediment to an accurate diagnosis. Even in 2010 men are far more likely to receive a more timely diagnoses of MS than are women even though women are roughly two times more likely to have MS. This is due, in part, to the fact that males appear to suffer more severe symptoms earlier in the disease process than do women. Of course, today we know that depression is often associated with conditions such as MS, far more frequently than with other chronic and debilitating diseases.

On January 14, 1963 I entered the psychiatric unit of North Carolina Memorial Hospital at the University of North Carolina in Chapel Hill. The Morganton psychiatrist who had been treating me for eight months felt I should prepare to remain in the hospital until I was no longer a danger to myself. Just weeks prior to this hospitalization I wrote the following poem.

Gyre

The corridor of glee is haunting me.
The laughing door with hidden knob
Cheerfully my soul would rob
Of sanity.
The curling lip upon the mask
Sneering lewdly takes to task
Integrity.
For gentle mirth's to laughter grown
And to the nodding world has shown
My mockery.
Would I were blessed to be at rest
In unity.

Morganton, North Carolina
November 1962

The poem that follows was written seven months earlier during my ten day hospitalization over the Easter holidays.

Easter Asylum

In April dawn comes early
And with it, peace.
The terrors of the night have ceased,
Stark phantoms soothed away
By slender clouds of dawn.
The world and I are one,
In unity complete.
Now no tortured ambivalence,
No taunting-voiced insistence
That all is lost.
For I have waked revitalized
To now behold with hopeful eyes
My world washed clean
With honest tears.

Butner State Hospital, NC
Easter 1962

CHAPTER FIVE: "CHILDREN, GO WHERE I SEND THEE"

Charlotte, North Carolina to Phoenix, Arizona: 1964

Towards the end of a six month hospitalization at N.C. Memorial Hospital, Steve and I came to the painful decision that due to the severity and complexity of my medical situation, divorce was the best option for Steve, for our three children and for me. This painful step was one my physicians strongly recommended. They predicted that without it, my survival was at best uncertain. During my last six weeks at N.C. Memorial my psychiatric treatment centered on helping me prepare for day-to-day existence that would not include my husband and children.

Steve and I planned for his parents to pick up the children in Auburndale and then drive them to Morganton. I would return to Morganton for approximately one month. While helping the children adjust to being back home, I would then find a housekeeper who could care for the children while Steve continued as a designer with Drexel Furniture.

Back in Morganton, while attempting to reestablish the routine the children had once enjoyed, I was acutely aware I needed to begin searching for the housekeeper who would not merely provide the children's and Steve's meals, perform laundry chores and other household duties but, far more importantly, would also give the children the tender care they needed and deserved. They had already endured far too much disruption in their young lives.

Yet, each day as I passed by the telephone, I postponed calling the Unemployment Office in Morganton. As I neared the beginning of my second week back home the anxiety of having made no attempt to find a housekeeper finally outweighed my anxiety over setting in motion events that would inevitably result in my separation from Steve and the children. Discussing and planning divorce from Steve and separation from the children was hard enough. Taking the necessary first step towards finding my replacement was proving incredibly difficult. I could barely get through each day as I contemplated what must be done.

On a Tuesday morning in early July I put Colin down for a brief nap while Steve and Ashley played in the back yard. It was a few minutes after 10:00 AM when I debated whether to take the laundry down to the washing machine in the basement or make the telephone call I'd been avoiding. Each night my last prayer was for strength to take this momentous first step. Each day ambivalence overcame me. Pausing by the telephone with a basket of laundry in my arms, one part of me argued, "Start the laundry and *then* make the call." Another part of me insisted, "Do it now! Do it now!"

The employment counselor who answered the phone listened without interruption to my request.

"We need a housekeeper who is good with small children ages 18 months to six years. We need her to work from 7:00 AM until 6:00 PM, Monday through Friday. We can pay between $15 and $20 each week. And if at all possible, I'd prefer that she is Catholic."

After a prolonged silence the gentleman responded. "Ma'am, I don't think there's much of a chance that anyone will be willing to work those hours for so little money regardless of religion. And I don't believe we have many Catholics here in Morganton." He did take down my name, address and phone number. And he did say he would contact me if anyone seemed interested in the position. I was quite certain I would never hear from him again.

After again stressing how important it was to find a housekeeper and asking that he do his very best on our behalf, I picked up the laundry basket. As I opened the door to the basement stairs I uttered a desperate prayer.

"Dear God, if it is your will for me to leave as planned, you will have to find someone wonderful to care for the children. And if I don't find a housekeeper, then I will know it is Your will that I remain here and that You will somehow enable me to do so." Laundry basket in hand, I then began descending the basement stairs. I had reached only the third or fourth step when the telephone rang. When I answered the phone I heard a gentle, accented voice.

"Mrs. Leonard, this is Mrs. Lovelace. The man at the Unemployment Office told me to call you. He said he had just spoken with you and that you really need a housekeeper."

Mrs. Lovelace then mentioned she'd gotten several busy signals that morning each time she dialed the Unemployment Office. In our conversation I also learned she was the mother of eight children, was from Hawaii and had married an American serviceman stationed there after the war. Her husband was a Morganton native.

"Oh," Mrs. Lovelace added. " I almost forgot. The man at the Unemployment Office told me to be sure and let you know I am a Catholic!"

While I was uttering my prayer of surrender and placing this painfully momentous decision about leaving my family totally in God's hands, Mrs. Lovelace was patiently redialing the telephone. And in North Carolina—the state with the smallest ratio of Catholics per capita—God had even fulfilled my request for a Catholic housekeeper!

Throughout the ensuing years God's prompt response to my heartfelt plea for assistance in finding a housekeeper continued to provide much needed comfort not only to my children but also to me. Between July 1963 and August 1964 I underwent two additional hospitalizations. The second hospitalization involved a sudden onset of severe upper back pain. Orthopedists in Charlotte, North Carolina urged that I move to a hot, dry climate, warning I would be confined to a wheelchair if I remained in the east where there were major fluctuations in barometric pressure.

With great reluctance I made another move. This move placed 2,200 miles between me and my children. I bade them goodbye at their grandparents' Thomasville home on the bleak Tuesday afternoon of November 17, 1964.

Arriving in Phoenix, Arizona during Thanksgiving week I felt isolated and unmoored—far removed from my children and everything that was familiar to me including the lush green or brilliant fall foliage of the Carolina countryside. In addition to the physical pain that intensified as each breath moved my ribs, the pain of grief weighed heavily on my heart. There were countless nights when sleep totally escaped me. Or if able to fall asleep, I would awaken in a few hours with a pounding heart and a litany of questions resounding in my mind.

"How on earth could I have left the man I loved and the three children whom I adored and who needed me?" I had yet to find work. How was I going to survive? Had I made dreadful decisions and ruined my children's lives and as well as Steve's and also mine? Yet one powerful memory offered a balm to the anxiety, self-judgment and almost paralyzing depression I experienced during the hours that many refer to as "the dark night of the soul." Only the memory of that July morning in 1963 comforted me as did my memories of all that had preceded Mrs. Lovelace's telephone call to me.

In Morganton I had prayed each night, "Oh Lord, Thy will be done. Give me the wisdom to discern it and the courage and strength to accomplish it."

I recalled my request that God provide an unambiguous sign regarding whether I should leave or stay. If He wanted me to leave He would have to provide a housekeeper for the children, a distinct improbability given how little we could pay for an 11 hour work day. God's response to my prayer had been immediate and unambiguous. God sent my family an angel in the form of Mrs. Lovelace to provide my children the love they needed.

No matter how much I missed the children, through God's striking, coincidental guidance I recognized He had clearly indicated the path He wished me to follow. Throughout the next eight years— and during my blackest moments—this memory of His intervention served as my life preserver. It helped me move forward with faith that God's plan was the best for everyone in our small family, including me.

My last image of my three children in the front yard of their grandparents' home was both emblazoned in my mind's eye and also accessible in a photograph taken that afternoon. A year later on Thanksgiving Day 1965 in Arizona I attempted to cope with my grief by composing a poem.

November Mourning

It was in November I saw my children last:
Stephan rolling in the leaves,
Ashley sitting on the grass.

I saw the lake—their father's lake—
Where many years before
He and I in love had lain
And dreamed our dreams devoid of pain.
Childlike was our faith and limited our vision;
Innocent our hearts of deeds
Dictating this decision.

It was in November I saw my children last:
Colin's laughter called to me
As he ran across the grass.
He did not know me as his mother
How could he remember
Eleven months of infancy,
Our only year together?

It was in November I saw the children last:
Two boys tumbling in the leaves,
One little girl upon the grass.

It was in November I saw three children last
And now, except in haunting dreams,
Motherhood has passed.

Thanksgiving 1965
Phoenix, Arizona

The Lord is *near to those who have a broken heart,*
And saves such as have a contrite spirit.

Psalm 34:18

☙

By January 1966 I had lived in Phoenix for 26 challenging months. I arrived in Phoenix weighing only 82 pounds. Three different Phoenix orthopedists confirmed the diagnosis the Charlotte physicians had made. I was suffering from ankylosing spondylitis (AS) which today is considered a form of rheumatoid arthritis. In 1964 it was described as producing a rigid, "bamboo spine." At the time of my diagnosis AS was considered incurable and generally untreatable. I was told eventually my entire spine would fuse and I would face the ground. One doctor suggested I opt for a surgical fusion, choosing whether to be fused in a sitting or in a standing position.

"If you opt to be fused in a sitting position you will at least be able to drive a car, but you will be confined to a wheelchair." Instinctively I chose to forego another spinal fusion and decided to place my trust in God. I prayed that if it were His will, He would spare me the most crippling effects of AS.

My osteopath stressed I must not work eight hours daily hunched over a typewriter. Even had I tried to do so, I discovered I would not have been hired as a secretary. My former exceptional typing and shorthand skills had deteriorated markedly and I now could type no faster than 29 correct words per minute.

The pain from the AS was severe. Every time I breathed it hurt. The one drug that gave me the most relief was butazolodin, but I developed blood dyscrasias which precluded long term use of this drug. Occasionally orthopedists would inject my back nerves with Novocain and prednisone. This procedure provided only temporary relief but any relief was most welcome.

Desperate for work I scoured the Help Wanted ads. I kept noticing an ad for sales personnel for Eterna 5 Light Bulbs. The ad stated that only the physically handicapped need apply. Curious, I called the number given in the newspaper. I doubted I would be considered sufficiently handicapped to qualify for employment. The supervisor quizzed me regarding my physical problems. I told him I had a spinal fusion when I was 16.

"A spinal fusion does not qualify as a handicap," he stated firmly.

"What about ankylosing spondylitis?" I asked.

"Oh, that definitely qualifies. Please come on down and let's see what I can do for you."

I immediately experienced two strong, conflicting emotions: profound relief that I qualified for employment accompanied by a frisson of stomach-churning fear because a disembodied voice on the phone had just confirmed my status as a handicapped person.

That afternoon I made my way to a small single-story building located in an industrial complex in downtown Phoenix near the railroad tracks. The scene that greeted me included four rows of five three-sided cubicles, each containing a desk top on which rested a telephone and multiple sheets torn from the Phoenix metropolitan residential telephone directory. Tacked to the particle board that faced each employee was a sales script. We were to read the script verbatim to any adult who answered the phone. It was printed in large type. The supervisor asked me to read the script to him and then showed me to my cubicle and gave me my supply of White Pages from which I was to make my calls that day.

The sound of more than 20 voices produced a deafening cacophony as men and women read aloud from the sales pitch. No one read at the same pace and the result was jarring and confusing, reminding me of the bedlam I had experienced during my ten-day hospitalization in the state mental hospital in Butner, North Carolina when an abrupt cessation of prednisone coupled with post-partum depression triggered thoughts of suicide.

The scene at Eterna 5 required intense concentration in order to shut out the surrounding voices. The visual impact of so many obviously handicapped individuals disturbed me profoundly at that stage of my illness as did the interminable din of their voices. Wheelchairs, walkers, and canes were everywhere. I viewed them as harbingers of what lay ahead for me. My interview with the supervisor included instructions that I demonstrate my ability to read the script tacked up on the board in each cubicle. He seemed pleased with my reading and told me to report for work the next day.

My relief at having a job and income—minimum hourly wage plus commissions on sales that exceeded a set quota for the week—barely surpassed the distress I experienced while working with others who were so visibly handicapped. It was difficult for me to adjust to the idea that I belonged in this group. I do not recall how many phone calls I placed my first day at Eterna 5. What I *do* vividly recall was how distressed I felt.

I remember silently vowing to myself, "If I have to spend another day much less the rest of my life doing this for a living I won't survive!" When I shared my thoughts and feeling with the supervisor he became agitated.

"Now just hold on! A few minutes ago I called our corporate offices when I saw how many bulbs you'd already sold and that was before you added five more bulbs to your day's total. They verified you have just broken the Eterna 5 record by selling more bulbs in one day than any other Eterna 5 sales associate has ever sold."

Reluctantly I promised my supervisor I would think about my decision overnight. The next morning, following a sleepless night, I phoned the supervisor who again pleaded with me to return to work. However, desperate as I was to find work, I knew I needed to find a job that offered work that I would find more intellectually demanding, work that would be more meaningful to me and a job with co-workers who were not such vivid reminders that I was now disabled despite my earlier efforts to overcome my physical limitations.

Fortunately I did find a temporary job for the holiday season. The Salvation Army ran newspaper advertisements offering residents in Phoenix and the surrounding cities an opportunity to contribute food, toys and clothing for inclusion in holiday baskets. I found this work to be meaningful even though it did also involve telephone solicitation.

As January 1, 1965 loomed nearer and my days of employment at the Salvation Army dwindled, I again experienced extreme anxiety attacks. These awakened me every night around 1:00 AM. I would huddle in the bathroom of the small apartment I shared with a friend. By 5:00 A.M. I often fell into an exhausted sleep from which I would again awaken at 7:00 AM with the same knot in my stomach and persistent diarrhea. My prayers continued for improved health and a job I could hold on to.

Shortly after New Year's Day my prayers were answered. The state unemployment office sent me to interview for a position as a receptionist for a child development center. Chris, the office manager, was a delightful woman whose bright smile and kind eyes put me at ease. Chris's obvious scoliosis also put me at ease and I shared with her that I had undergone surgery for a similar condition. Her dramatic curvature was the result of surgical treatment of tuberculosis. Chris did not offer me the job that day, but she did agree I could contact her in a few days to see if she and the center's executive director had made a decision regarding me. Despite my concerns that I would be considered a pest, I did make two calls during the next ten days. At the end of the second call Chris spoke the words I had hoped to hear.

"Well, come on in to work tomorrow and let's see how things go."

It was such a relief to have a job. Earning $280 each month seemed a king's ransom compared to earning nothing at all. I threw myself into the work which I found interesting. This treatment center was affiliated with St. Luke's Hospital through a federal grant from the National Institute of Mental Health. The center used a multidisciplinary team approach and employed clinical social workers, psychologists and psychiatrists for the evaluation and treatment of emotionally disturbed children. There was also a school for children who could not function in a public school. These children received both individual and group therapy and their parents received group therapy as well.

My job was to manage calls on four incoming lines, schedule appointments and maintain the Case Control process so that no child became lost in the intake and assessment processes which included an Intake Interview with a social worker, an MSW; a psychological evaluation of the child coupled with psychological testing of the parents; and a possible psychiatric evaluation of the child if the psychologist deemed it necessary. During a subsequent Staff Conference the entire professional staff developed a treatment plan for the child and its parents. All family members were then assigned to the therapists deemed most appropriate with respect to the child's and the parents' diagnoses.

While it was difficult for me to encounter small children on a daily basis—ones that often were the same ages as my own children—I enjoyed feeling useful and part of a team. The center's director told me that as the receptionist, I was the first person to whom parents of troubled children spoke about the problems in their family. He encouraged me to listen with an understanding ear and a compassionate heart.

"But don't try to solve their problems or give advice. Just listen and then schedule an Intake Interview with an MSW."

While my back pain persisted I learned to work through it as best I could. When the pain was intolerable I received nerve block injections that often brought immediate yet impermanent relief. Then in late August 1965 one of these injections nearly cost me my life. A new orthopedist managed to collapse my lung when he miscalculated just how thin an atrophied back muscle was as a result of polio. He missed the nerve he intended to inject and the needle penetrated and collapsed my right lung. As a result of this medical misadventure I spent a week in the hospital following a thoracotomy during which I suffered cardiac arrest. Even though I returned to my receptionist duties three weeks sooner than my chest surgeon recommended, on my 28th birthday I found myself out of a job. I was clearing out my desk when Dr. George Dee, a psychologist spoke to me.

"Lynn, you need a college education. Here is the name of a friend of mine, Marvin Deuring, who is a counselor with the Arizona Department of Vocational Rehabilitation. He's expecting your call and is confident he can help you get the education you need and deserve."

Dr. Dee had survived the Bataan Death March. Like Chris, the office manager, he had also been treated in a TB sanitarium in

Phoenix and, after many years, he also underwent a thoracoplasty to arrest his tuberculosis. During his lifetime I am confident George blessed countless individuals because that was God's plan for him. How blessed was I to encounter George Dee and to be one of the many people he helped.

Only since I began writing Not By Chance have I stopped to consider the intricate way in which God wove the tapestry of my life at this critical juncture. At the child development center I became one of three employees with marked scoliosis. Here God guided each of us who was experiencing physical challenges to use our personal pain to alleviate the pain of others. Years later I encountered the term "wounded healers" and recognized that George, Chris and I identified ourselves that way. That was God's plan, for each of us to be of service to others.

As I write this I ponder the 23-year span of history that culminated in January 1965 and brought together Dr. George Dee, Chris the office manager, and me. George Dee had survived the infamous 1942 Bataan Death March. On two occasions George shared with me how determined he had been to survive the extreme deprivation of the Japanese prisoner of war camp in which he lived for nearly four years until the war finally ended. Sick with tuberculosis, George then wound up far from home in Phoenix for treatment of his tuberculosis. Chris was a Midwesterner who also had been sent to Phoenix for years of treatment in a TB sanitarium. And I was a divorced mother of three who had also been sent to Phoenix from North Carolina for my major health challenges.

God had arranged for the three of us to be in place at Jane Wayland Center where each of us could play our ordained role. I suspect a less physically challenged office manager than Chris would have been far less likely to hire a physically challenged receptionist like me whose frail frame made my serious health challenges readily apparent. And certainly a hale and hearty psychologist might never have thought to refer me to the Arizona Department of Vocational Rehabilitation for assistance in obtaining a college education.

Only God's intricate plan could bring together all three of us as employees of that same small child development center in what even then was a fair-sized city. If any of us had been employed elsewhere I seriously doubt that I would ever have been able to attend Arizona

State University. Thus what had seemed at first to be a catastrophe—becoming unemployed on my 28th birthday— proved instead to be providential. A door slammed shut upon my work as a receptionist and simultaneously, a door opened up to the path God intended for me with respect to education and profession.

⟨⟨

Two days later Marvin Deuring visited me during my brief hospitalization for reactive depression. Following a series of physical and psychological assessments, the Arizona Department of Vocational Rehabilitation officially certified me as disabled. They would pay my tuition at Arizona State University, purchase my books and also provide a $90 monthly stipend throughout my undergraduate years while I worked to obtain a bachelor's degree in English. I was amazed to learn I would also receive Economic Opportunity Grants and other monetary awards plus federal student loans. At this juncture, I did not experience a viscerally negative reaction to realizing I was, in fact, disabled. The opportunity to gain a college education went a long way towards removing the "sting" of that label and condition.

After the university deducted my tuition and book allowance from the total amount of my financial aid, I would net more disposable income than I had earned as a receptionist. This financial assistance would begin in June, 1966 when I would attend the first session of summer school. All I needed to do in the meantime was earn enough money to survive. For the next five months I worked as a professional babysitter, an irony that did not escape me. My gratitude to God and the state of Arizona was unbounded.

By early May I was in a celebratory mood as I donned the white uniform the Lullaby Guild require me to wear anytime I babysat children in a motel or hotel. That lovely evening I was sitting with three children ages 12, 9 and 5 in their parents' suite at The Ranch House Motel on Central Avenue when an horrendous noise of screeching brakes and colliding metal reached my ears. As I looked out the ground floor window of the room where my charges and I were playing cards, I saw a dreadful scene. A young man lay in the middle of the road beside two cars that had collided head-on. Admonishing the twelve-year-old girl to lock the door behind me and open to no one other than me, I dashed out the door and walked quickly towards the wreck. Once there I checked the pulse of the individual who lay on the pavement and then moved to check the condition of the young man who was behind the steering wheel of the other vehicle.

This second accident victim was pinned by the steering wheel against his seat. Somehow I managed to pull the steering column away from him, free him and then drag him from the car and out of the street. I then placed him in a prone position and instructed the conscious man to lie still. I had barely accomplished this when a young man arrived.

"I'm a fourth year medical student. Tell me what to do!"

"Check both guys for signs of shock and then see if the motel people will lend us blankets. And let's find some way to elevate their feet. Make certain someone has called for ambulances." Even as I responded I wondered why a fourth year medical student was asking me what to do. Then as I moved to check on the first victim I heard a familiar voice.

"Gal, what are you doing dragging someone from a wrecked car? I just certified you as disabled?" Marvin Deuring demanded.

After the ambulances and police had come and gone, Mr. Deuring and I chatted briefly. "I could hardly believe my eyes when I spotted you pulling that man from the vehicle. Then I heard the bystander identify himself as a med student and ask what you wanted him to do. And by golly, you didn't hesitate for even a second. You just told him what to do and he did it." Mr. Deuring and I eventually concluded the med student deferred to me because he thought my white uniform indicated I was an RN.

Once again I found myself experiencing a remarkable set of coincidences. I cannot begin to calculate the likelihood that I, a new Voc Rehab student, would be babysitting in a motel in metropolitan Phoenix in front of which a two car accident would occur just as my Voc Rehab counselor also happened upon the scene. There were at least 75 other Phoenix motels in which I might have been babysitting that evening.

Also, from most other rooms in the motel in which I was babysitting that evening, it is likely I would have even been completely unaware of the collision on Central Avenue. And Marvin Deuring might have happened by the scene either minutes earlier, minutes later or not at all. In fact, that evening Mr. Deuring mentioned that Central Avenue was not his accustomed route home. He happened to be returning to his office on Central from an appointment in north Phoenix prior to getting on the freeway for his 30 minute commute to Mesa in the southeast valley.

In May 1966 I fear these coincidences only caused me to shake my head. As I write these words in 2010, I now recognize there were several messages of which I then was unaware. First, however physically challenged I might be, God gave me the capacity to respond to the needs of others. Second, I was able to manage well in challenging situations. Third, others saw me as a leader and placed confidence in me.

As my life unfolded over the coming years, the themes of this specific coincidence appeared repeatedly. Without my awareness, God's coincidences were revealing attributes our Lord had placed within me— attributes He was burnishing in the crucible of my challenging life.

And we know that all things work together for good to those who love God, to those who are called according to His purpose.

Romans 8:28

CHAPTER SIX: SCALING MOUNT ACADEMIA

Arizona State University, Tempe, Arizona, 1966-1972

For the next four years I pursued a B.A. degree in English. While I could not believe my good fortune to be paid to read and study, my undergraduate years were challenging. Poor balance made my daily life frightening almost every minute I was in a vertical position. This problem had first surfaced when Colin was eight months old but had abated during my six months as an inpatient at N.C. Memorial Hospital. During my first summer school session at ASU this balance problem returned with a vengeance. I frequently fell backwards and to my left. Marvin Deuring arranged for me to see a neurologist but my balance issues continued. The doctor suggested I use crutches to steady me but I needed one arm free to pull the shopping cart I used for hauling my books around ASU's extensive campus so I used a single crutch.

Even using one crutch I fell frequently, often several times in one day. Following a small car accident I experienced severe pain and extreme exhaustion, I spent a week in the hospital. I spent the next three months on doctor-ordered bed rest. However, after borrowing notes from classmates I did manage to take both the mid-term and final exams. When Spring term began I signed up for a full course load, but in March I underwent a hysterectomy for early stage cervical cancer. I lost all but one hour's credit for a directed reading course in English Literature. After attending both summer sessions, by August

1967 I was indeed grateful to have earned enough credits to achieve classification as a sophomore.

During the remainder of my undergraduate years I was able to attend only 50% of my classes. In addition to pain, balance and fatigue, vision presented an additional challenge. After only 30 minutes of study my eyes could no longer focus and I then needed to rest my eyes or nap for ten minutes. In the spring of my junior year and while hospitalized in the Student Health Center, my physician told me I was too seriously ill to remain at ASU and burden a roommate with my care. He urged me to return to Florida so that my parents could provide for me. I mentioned I had been sent to Arizona by orthopedists who insisted I needed a dry, desert climate. What I did not know at that time and would not learn for another ten years was that the neurologist to whom Voc Rehab had sent me in 1967 had made an additional diagnosis of my condition. Not until 1979 would I learn what that diagnosis was and the future it foretold.

Several of my English professors befriended me. One voiced genuine concern about my future. "You may be able to graduate with honors while missing half your classes, but who will hire you and retain you if you aren't able teach half of your classes?"

Margaret's concern was certainly valid. I had pondered the same question throughout my college career. Awakened during the night by anxiety and panic I would nearly surrender to the negative implications of that concern. I would ask myself, "Who are you kidding? You'll never be able to hold a job. The State of Arizona is wasting money to educate you for work you will never be able to do!"

Committing my fears and feelings to verse released me from the prison in which they'd held me.

Intimate Enemy

Long have I known pain.
A lifetime we have been companions.
In daylight we have struggled,
My sore strength against my body's vise.
At night I've whimpering lain
Playing the waiting game

While watching for the dawn.
Others have struggled, watched and waited
Long before me. Multitudes do battle daily
With our common foe. That is no comfort.
The brave words they have uttered
Do not bolster me. They leap forth from
The page as barbs to
Failing flesh and flagging will.
I've won no glorious victory over pain.
There is no glamour in my endurance.
Yet I survive from day to day
Bare master of my lethargy.

1969: Arizona State University,
Tempe, Arizona

Then one night as I lay wake worrying about how I could retain employment given my physical challenges, an incontrovertible truth occurred to me. "Lynn, only one thing is certain. If you don't complete your education, you definitely will not be able to support yourself. Push on! Trust in Him!" Following this revelation I recommitted myself to completing my degree. I experienced renewed and strengthened faith in the loving God who had placed me upon this path and brought me so far.

Then in December 1969 my pain, balance, fatigue and vision problems intensified. On one particular day I fell 16 times. A new pair of glasses that Voc Rehab had paid for in September no longer enabled me to read. A second visit to the ophthalmologist left me totally exasperated. As he again began the tedious process of trying one corrective lens after another he commanded, "This time pay more attention. Try to be more explicit about which adjustment is an improvement and which is not!"

At the beginning of the second semester of my senior year one of my professors prayed for me during a conference in his office. He asked if I would allow him to send a woman to my apartment, one who was well known for her healing touch. After her visit I did not experience any immediate or dramatic reduction in pain or increase in energy or improved vision. However, shortly after her visit I decided to try two different approaches to deal with my pain and other conditions. I began forming mental images of my pain in which I moved it down through my arms and out my fingertips. At other times I imagined the most painful areas in my thoracic spine as being a deep magenta towards which I would direct a bright healing light. In my most successful approach I formed the image of myself in miniature, sitting inside that angry magenta cauldron, much as Daniel walked in the fiery furnace. As I sat there, I acknowledged the reason for my pain.

"Thank you for your pain signals. However, I am very aware there is a problem. Therefore you can be less strident with these signals."

That shift in focus—*away* from anger at my body in which I felt it was my enemy that minute-by-minute betrayed me and inflicted pain and fatigue, daily falls and blurred vision—and *towards* thanking my body for doing its job—began producing a subtle but consistent lessening of my pain and a reduction in other problems with balance and vision.

The next change in my regimen was more dramatic. All of my doctors had again been adamant. "Don't do anything when you are running a fever, when your joints are hot and inflamed. Do not exercise at these times."

In compliance with their instructions, I was inactive most all the time because I routinely ran a low-grade fever with temperature of 99^0-100.2^0. By the early spring of 1970 I was so frustrated that I concluded, "If I'm hurting like Hades from doing nothing, I'd rather hurt because I'm doing something!"

I then spent $60 on a combination rowing machine and tilt board and began exercising on a daily basis. I began to feel much better. As my pain diminished I also decided to begin reducing the amount of Darvon-65 my orthopedist had prescribed for the past six years. He had assured me Darvon was not addictive but I was not convinced. I gradually reduced and then eliminated my use of this product.

While there is no objective proof, no one will ever persuade me that these new approaches that I began using during the last semester of my senior year were not the result of God empowering that healer's touch. The healer sent to me by a professor was a woman whose countenance radiated the Holy Spirit. But at the time of her ministrations I had been so intent on experiencing an immediate response to her touch that I confess I initially did not recognize how effective her touch had been. It was many years before I recognized that the Holy Spirit had utilized her touch to introduce a remarkable sequence of healing actions in my life. Through this healer's touch the Holy Spirit inspired me to try the mental and physical approaches that then produced such remarkable improvements in my health.

At the time I graduated from ASU my life journey had already included several striking instances of God guiding my path through His coincidences. The approaches I used in my senior year were, of course, similar to those I'd been inspired to use 15 years earlier—approaches that enabled me to cope with pain and manage to walk despite the medical prognosis I would spend my life in a wheelchair. I had regained the ability to walk by listening to the inspiring music "I'll Walk with God" while imagining how it had felt to walk and run.

Fifteen years later, during that last semester of my senior year, I had prayerfully set aside my panic about being unable to hold a job due to the excessive absences my physical condition would likely cause. Once again I then experienced the powerful benefits of uniting positive thoughts of gratitude with my body and spirit. As graduation approached I began to reconsider my career path. I remembered all the various professionals who had helped me with my psychological and emotional problems when depression held me in its nearly lethal grip. After prayerful consideration, I decided to pursue the new 60 hour Master of Counseling degree at Arizona State University rather than continue in English for both master and doctorate degrees.

On the warm May afternoon of my graduation in 1970 with a B.A. in English, Dr. C. Gilbert Wrenn, Professor Emeritus in ASU's Counseling Department and a renowned author in the counseling field, hired me as his Research Assistant to work with him on his next book, *The World of the Contemporary Counselor* which the publisher, Houghton-Mifflin, had just commissioned.

HOW SWEET IT IS!

Author's 1970 Graduation
Arizona State University

With the monthly $200 stipend Dr. Wrenn would pay me and my student loans, I would be able to afford my graduate education. I began work with Dr. Wrenn the following Monday. He and Mrs. Wrenn were leaving for a tour of Eastern Bloc universities where he would be a Guest Lecturer. Dr. Wrenn instructed me to meet him and Mrs. Wrenn at the Thomas Mall in Phoenix. As we sipped iced tea at Diamond's Department store he handed me a cardboard box containing hundreds of newspaper clippings. Atop these clippings was a one page list of chapter headings for his new book. During his two month absence I was to select one of the 12 chapter topics, conduct research on that topic guided by the tenor of the newspaper clippings, journal articles and any additional material my reading of pertinent books generated. I was to distill the information and commit it to paper in a triple-spaced format.

Dr. Wrenn insisted I work no more than 20 hours each week but I found it impossible challenge to limit my hours. I had the use of Dr. Wrenn's private office located in the basement of ASU's Carl Hayden Library. I also enjoyed free photocopying privileges and assistance from the Reference Librarians. In other words, I found myself in a English major's paradise. I could but marvel and give thanks to God for my good fortune. Six months later during an afternoon tea break at his home, Dr. Wrenn shared some surprising news. I had been the only student who responded to his posted ad for a Research Assistant.

"Lynn, I confess I was disappointed to have no choice in the matter. In the past, graduate students vied to work with me. In addition, I was troubled by the fact that you were just beginning your studies in counseling and equally concerned that your background in English would prove a hindrance." Dr. Wrenn then smiled and his blue eyes twinkled.

"But, my dear, I am so grateful I had no choice in the matter. You are precisely the right person for this book. God knew better than I just what I needed." God had also known precisely what I needed! In Gilbert Wrenn and his wonderful wife, Kathleen, I found not only mentors but dear and faithful friends as I later attempted to convey in my poem, "The Greeners," in Chapter Twelve.

In August 1972 I received the Master of Counseling degree from ASU. During that summer while Dr. and Mrs. Wrenn were in South Africa where he lectured at the University of South Africa at Durban, I completed all my editorial duties for *The World of the Contemporary Counselor*. When Dr. Wrenn received 50 advanced copies he presented me with one on which he had inscribed the flyleaf. As I read his kind words I also discovered he had listed me as Research Associate rather than Research Assistant. My name appeared on the title page immediately below his name in a pt. size almost as large. A few months later when Dr. Wrenn returned from lecturing in London, he chuckled in delight while informing me the Bodleian Library listed me as co-author in their card catalogue.

On October 14, 1972 I paid a visit to the Research Librarians at the Hayden Library where I had worked so happily for Dr. Wrenn. I still had found no job and was growing increasingly uneasy. These competent and caring women had been so kind and gracious to me during the two years I was in and out of the 'stacks,' relying upon their knowledge and expertise. I simply wanted to connect with them once more. When I appeared in the Research Department on the 4th floor, they greeted me enthusiastically and asked where I was working. I replied I had not yet found work but mentioned I had attended the first Advisory Committee meeting of the new Division on Aging of Catholic Charities. In fact, I had been elected Chairman of the Advisory Committee.

"At least I'm meeting people who are interested in the field of gerontology. Who knows where these contacts may lead? Unfortunately, it is not a paid position. Cele Halas in the Counseling Department sent me to the meeting hoping I'd be hired as the director of their new Retired Senior Volunteer Program but the two key staff positions with RSVP were already filled."

Miriam, a librarian to whom I had grown especially close, called me aside.

"Lynn, would you mind if I prayed for you and your job search right now?"

I thanked her and told her how much I would appreciate her prayers. Miriam led me to a more private area where we stopped near one of the larger photocopy machines and bowed our heads. Miriam prayed that I find a job where I could be useful. I then headed back home feeling much encouraged.

When I arrived home I went back to my study and began making a new list of agencies to contact. I had already met with both the administrator and director of nursing at Boswell Hospital in Sun City. Because Boswell was primarily a geriatric hospital with twice the customary mortality rate of general hospitals, I had encouraged them to consider hiring me to provide supportive counseling for the nursing staff as well as individual and/or group support for patients' family members. Thus far, they were still considering my proposal. As I attempted to boost my courage to contact the administrators at Boswell Hospital, once again I prayed.

"Lord, you know my need. Please use me where I am needed and where you would have me be."

I had resumed studying the Help Wanted section of the Arizona Republic when the sudden ringing of the telephone startled me. Fr. Otte, Director of the Division on Aging, was on the phone.

"Lynn, the woman we hired as RSVP director just resigned and she suggested we offer the job to you. The pay is very low for someone with your educational qualifications but we believe we can manage a major raise in pay within a few months."

Without a moment's hesitation, I accepted the position. Of course it meant resigning my unpaid position as chairman of the RSVP Advisory Committee, a resignation I was happy to tender. Once again, God's response to my prayer of acceptance of His divine will was immediate. I certainly also credited the intercessory prayer of Miriam, the librarian, just an hour earlier as another significant factor in the timely appearance of this job offer.

Looking back I marvel that I accepted the offer. I was to be paid a scant $6,000 annually—the exact salary Steve had earned on his first job right out of Pratt back in 1960. I had a two year masters degree and was $7,200 in debt from my educational loans. At a minimum, my commute from home in Tempe to Northern Boulevard in north central Phoenix would be 35-40 minutes in each direction.

Even so, I did not hesitate to consider whether or not this was the job for me. I had prayed, the librarian had prayed, Cele Halas whom I knew only slightly had pointed me in the direction of Catholic Charities which in turn led to my election as chairman of the RSVP advisory committee and then to my appointment as RSVP Program Director.

I was not about to question where God had sent me!

For we are His workmanship,
created in Christ Jesus for good works,
which God prepared beforehand that
we should walk in them.

Ephesians 3:10

CHAPTER SEVEN: THE BEST OF TIMES
Phoenix to Philadelphia & New Orleans: 1972

T wo months after receiving the Master of Counseling degree from Arizona State University and the culmination of my work with Dr. Wrenn, I became program director of the Retired Senior Volunteer Program for Maricopa County. Catholic Charities' new Division on Aging sponsored the program. I had been elected chairman of the RSVP Advisory Board on a Thursday and then hired on Saturday as its inaugural RSVP director. When I undertook that role I had absolutely no experience with government grants and knew nothing about administering such a program. However, it did address my interest in gerontology and I learned quickly that the priest to whom I was responsible also had no experience with federal grants. However, Fr. Otte said he knew a wonderful woman in Philadelphia who was willing to open her home to me and tutor me regarding running a successful federal program sponsored by a Catholic agency. From her home I was to then to fly on to New Orleans where I would attend the first national meeting of RSVP directors. In December 1972 there were only 60 RSVP programs in the nation.

This trip was a white-knuckle experience for me. At nearly 35 years of age I had never gone off to one, much less two, unknown cities by myself. Having a new job about which no one seemed to know more than I was an unsettling experience. My flight to

Philadelphia would be my first time flying alone since my first ever flight—the one to Lawton via Atlanta and Dallas—the one in which the plane lost an engine. I tried mightily to lose myself in a mystery novel but my mind kept straying to myriad concerns about both my unknown hostess and my unclear job responsibilities. As my anxiety mounted I began to pray. The flight seemed interminable and despite my prayers, my panic was rising.

About 30 minutes out of Philadelphia the gentleman in the seat beside me struck up a conversation. I have never recalled how our conversation led me to mention that my parents lived in Florida, but this man asked what part of Florida they lived in. I replied it was a very small town in the lake region of central Florida, near Winter Haven.

"By any chance would that be Auburndale?" he asked. When I said it certainly was, he asked what street my parents lived on in Auburndale. When I said West Lake Avenue he became excited.

" I know West Lake Avenue quite well. I used to rent a room there in what had once been a doctor's residence on that same street. It was a big old white frame house, two stories with a garage apartment and several acres of green lawn that sloped down to a private, white sandy beach on Lake Ariana. It was the only two story home on West Lake down by the boat ramp. Do you know the house I mean?"

"I'm pretty certain I do. Do you recall the street number for the house you lived in?"

"As a matter of fact I do. I lived there for nearly a year back in 1954. The address was 309 West Lake Avenue."

Smiling and shaking my head I confided that my parents had bought that same house at 309 West Lake Avenue in May 1959 and that my husband and I, together with our two children, had lived there the summer after my folks purchased the home.

"My parents live there still!" I added.

MY PARENTS' LAKESIDE HOME

309 West Lake Avenue in Auburndale, Florida

Other details of that Philadelphia trip are missing from my memory bank. What I do clearly recall is how comforted I felt upon learning I was sitting next to a man who had once rented the very room my husband and I shared in my parents' home in a tiny town of 4,000 citizens in Auburndale, Florida. My anxiety simply drained away as I recalled Ethel Waters' inimitable rendition of "His eye is on the sparrow and I know He watches me."

I served as program director of RSVP for nearly three years. Then God guided me to suggest incorporating the Division on Aging as a sister, non-profit corporation to Catholic Charities under the auspices of The Roman Catholic Diocese of Phoenix. I was privileged to play an instrumental role in the design, development and administration of four multidisciplinary Adult Day Health Centers that provided milieu therapy to physically and/or mentally challenged senior citizens. In addition we developed two large homemaker/home health aide services, one for Maricopa County and one for the City of Phoenix and also a therapeutic recreation program for seniors. These facilities and programs provided a continuum of care for local seniors who needed assistance in order to live at home rather than in nursing homes

My career dreams came to fruition during these years. I had believed my ideal career would include teaching and writing as well as program design, development and administration. God blessed me with adjunct clinical appointments in two colleges at Arizona State University: the College of Nursing's graduate program and the Graduate School of Social Work. In addition, I was able to publish in the areas of Adult Day Health as well as Death and Dying. I am certain that the multidisciplinary approach I implemented in our agency's Adult Day Health Centers was the direct result

of the year I worked as the receptionist at the child development center where a multidisciplinary approach benefited all of their clients.

Looking back I now see how God's answer to my desperate pleas for a job in December 1964 and January 1965 provided far more than employment. For through my job at Jane Wayland Child Development Center I met Dr. Dee who played such an integral role in helping me obtain financial support for my college education. And it was at this same center that I learned the value of using a multidisciplinary team approach to address the needs of clients.

In 1973 life became even more abundant when Ashley and Colin came to live with me while their dad was getting resettled following a divorce from his second wife. When Steve Jr. came for a visit and all three of my children were with me for the first time since 1963, I experienced a happiness I had never thought possible. Steve Jr. and Colin eventually returned to live with or near their dad and his parents. Ashley graduated from high school in Mesa, Arizona and then entered the journalism program at Arizona State University.

For me these truly were the "best of times." I rejoiced that my health problems appeared to be past, that my children and I were reconnecting, and that God was allowing me to be of benefit to so many of His children.

> *You have turned for me*
> *my mourning into dancing;*
> *You have put off my sackcloth*
> *and clothed me with gladness,*
> *To the end that my glory may*
> *sing praise to You and not be silent.*
> *O Lord my God, I will give*
> *thanks to you forever.*
>
> **Psalm 30:11-12**

CHAPTER EIGHT: THE WORST OF TIMES
Tempe, Arizona: Spring, Summer & Fall 1979

Nine years of good health abruptly ended on April 29, 1979. Following lunch at a nearby Mexican restaurant where my work colleagues and I dined at noon each day, as I tried to exit the booth in which I had been sitting I discovered my legs would not support me. The pain I experienced reminded me of what I had experienced during my second pregnancy when I attempted to stand and felt extreme pain in the center of my pelvis. However, on this April day in 1979 I was not pregnant and I could not bear weight at all. A colleague whose father was a retired orthopedic surgeon drove me to the hospital near my Tempe home. Her father ordered an emergency consult with *Dr. Anthony. Early that evening he admitted me as an orthopedic patient. Prior to discharging me eight days later Dr. Anthony called for a neurological consult.

"I think you are hiding a lot of symptoms from me and perhaps even from yourself," Dr. Anthony stated as he accidentally launched his pen across my room. The neurologist, *Dr. Chastain, examined me on the day I was discharged from the hospital.

Early in May Ashley and I flew to North Carolina for my son Steve's wedding. Back in Phoenix on June 3, my daughter's 21st birthday, I kept an appointment with the orthopedist. With

---

*   This name is a pseudonym

glistening eyes Dr. Anthony imparted shocking news. He and the neurologist concurred I had amyotrophic lateral sclerosis—ALS— often also called Lou Gehrig's disease. After receiving this diagnosis I found myself out in the parking lot, standing next to my car, and with no awareness of how I had arrived there. I had a vague impression of the receptionist calling out "Mrs. Leonard!" as I bolted the doctor's office—if one can be said to "bolt" while using arm crutches. I needed to pick up Ashley at ASU because her car was being repaired following a recent accident.

While driving the length of Apache Boulevard from Mesa to ASU I began to shake violently.

From my years working in the Adult Day Health arena I knew about ALS and the hideous death it entailed. Over the weekend I went to the library to learn all I could about this dreadful disease. I discovered I had difficulty seeing words on the page I was reading. The cause of this difficulty was simple. As I read the shocking facts about ALS I involuntarily was shielding my eyes with my hand so that I was reading the page through my half-spread fingers. One physician's shocking statement sent me reeling outdoors in search of fresh air. He indicated that if he were ever diagnosed with ALS he would find an undetectable way to commit suicide in order to spare both his family and himself the anguish associated with ALS.

Late one evening my orthopedist returned my phone call. It was not an uplifting conversation. I had asked why he and the neurologist were not doing more to confirm their clinical ALS diagnosis. His voice was very gentle. "Lynn, we're not ordering a muscle biopsy. It's a painful procedure and we just don't want to spoil what little good time you have left."

Ashley was graduating in August. Above all, I desperately wanted her to settle somewhere else—with her father, with my mother or best of all with a suitable husband. I wanted Ashley anywhere but with me in Arizona where she would observe my decline and feel responsible for my care. My graduation gift to Ashley was a trip back to North Carolina to visit her friends, father, grandparents and younger brother followed by a trip down to Florida to visit her newly married older brother. Ashley would then come to my mother's home in Auburndale. There she planned to reconnect with a young man she had dated while a teenager. In my heart I hoped Ashley and he might discover how right they seemed for one another. Mother and I thought they had the promise of developing a lasting and loving relationship. While Ashley was in North Carolina my mother and I planned to take a short cruise to the Bahamas.

By the time I reached Mother's home in Auburndale and we boarded the cruise ship in Miami I was totally exhausted. Mother seemed to be in denial regarding the seriousness of my diagnosis and expected me to keep up with her onboard ship. All I wanted to do was sleep and rest. Among the other passengers was a group of US Postal Service workers from the Washington DC area. The women in this group were exceedingly sensitive to the disparity between Mother's needs and mine. Several of them engaged Mother in conversation and strolls on deck. One woman in particular was very sensitive and understanding.

"Child, don't feel you have to keep me company. You just sit here beside me and soak up God's sun and listen to the soothing sound of His endless sea." Decades later I still recall her tender care with profound appreciation.

The first night we were onboard I noticed a man in an electric scooter. He was accompanied by three women. Later I learned they were his wife and two grown daughters who still lived at home. He approached me and we began exchanging medical histories. He was an MS patient. His multiple sclerosis had been diagnosed when he was 41. He explained he had been confined to using a scooter for four years. In addition to the weakness in his legs, he explained he suffered from total urinary incontinence. On the second day of the cruise this man startled me with an incredible statement.

"If they found a cure for MS tomorrow I wouldn't take the cure. I'm collecting on three separate pensions and my wife and two daughters wait on me hand and foot. I don't have to work and I lack for nothing, So why would I want a cure?"

Without censoring my thoughts I retorted, "You've got lots more wrong with you than MS!" His attitude profoundly disturbed me.

For the rest of the cruise I found ways to avoid him. I'm ashamed to confess it did not even occur to me to pray for him.

At lunch the following day I had a rude awakening. I could not lift the full water pitcher beside me to pass it down to the person on my left. I could not believe my right arm was suddenly so weak. I had always prided myself on my upper body strength. Now I couldn't even hoist a water pitcher!

A woman who sat across the table from me caught my eye and we began to get acquainted with one another. She shared that she and her husband owned a farm in Iowa. This cruise was their first vacation in 27 years of marriage. After lunch she asked if I would join her on deck. We took a short walk together. Leaning on the rail as we both looked out on the vast ocean with its varied blues and greens, this sweet lady asked about my need for crutches. When I mentioned ALS she nodded and smiled sadly.

"That's my diagnosis, too. My doctors encouraged me to fulfill any dreams we had as soon as possible. Being from the Midwest where there's mostly only manmade ponds and certainly no oceans, we had always dreamed of taking a cruise. This was the only cruise we could afford."

Gazing out to sea I pondered the statistical odds of finding two ALS patients among 800 individuals taking a cruise to the Bahamas. I did not think the odds were very high, given the fact that ALS is a rare disease with fewer than 5,000 new diagnoses annually and no more than 20,000 total ALS patients in the US in 1979.

When we returned to Auburndale after the cruise and with hurricane warnings in effect, I decided to leave for Arizona a few days earlier than scheduled. Ashley remained at Mother's and the romance between her and Jordan (not his real name) appeared to be in full bloom. Back in Arizona I made an appointment to see my orthopedist. When I told him about my inability to hoist a water pitcher his response was immediate.

"Lynn, I need to turn you over to Dr. Chastain. He will follow you from here on out." Ten days later I met with Dr. Chastain for the second time.

"What brings you here?" he asked. When I recounted my new symptom—the sudden weakness in my dominant arm—and repeated Dr. Anthony's statement that he was turning my care over to him as the neurologist, Dr. Chastain's response was immediate and emphatic.

"Oh, no! Dr. Anthony's not going to saddle me with this by myself. You still have orthopedic problems!"

Chastain then ordered an EMG test to be followed by a muscle biopsy. After the EMG I received a call from Chastain's office asking that I meet with him the following day. When I entered his private office Dr. Chastain waved me to take a chair facing him across his desk. Leaning back in his black leather executive chair—hands and fingers forming a steeple—he intoned his pronouncement.

"Madam, I'm pleased to inform you that you do *not* have amyotrophic lateral sclerosis. You *do* have a progressive, degenerative neurological disorder of unknown etiology. It *will not* be necessary for you to see me again." He rose, shook my hand and in parting, volunteered he would be happy to make my medical records available to my future neurologist.

Dr. Chastain's words rang in my ears as I exited his office with a light heart and without a backward glance. Once home, I made a note regarding the words he had used to free me from the nightmare in which I'd lived for nearly six months. While a few people suggested I file a malpractice claim against the neurologist for the agony I experienced as the result of his misdiagnosis, I thought otherwise. I had just received my life back. God had blessed me abundantly.

Following the initial ALS diagnosis my prayers had been for courage to face the end I knew was awaiting me and for God to find some way to protect Ashley from witnessing it. I had never thought to pray for healing from ALS. Nor had I thought to question their diagnosis. Several months later Marvin Deuring, my former Vocational Rehab Counselor, phoned to say in his breathless manner that he had just heard I had ALS.

"Gal, you don't have ALS—what you have is MS! MS was diagnosed back in 1967 by the neurologist we sent you to when your balance and vision were so poor. I instructed the doc to withhold the

MS diagnosis from you. I didn't think you could handle a second dire diagnosis. You were doing so well at ASU and I just didn't want you to lapse into the deep depression that had plagued you for so many years." (Of course, today withholding a diagnosis would never occur.)

After that last office visit with Dr. Chastain I took a brief hiatus from "doctoring" as a dear Southern friend of mine termed it. However, within two months I was experiencing increased fatigue and hideously painful muscle spasms. My balance was now worse than ever. In addition, one of my secretaries mentioned I had begun omitting numerous letters within words in the grant proposals or letters I'd give her to type. And when I tried to read, the printed material looked as if someone had removed letters in the middle of words with ink eradicator. Eating had become an exhausting process no matter how hungry I was. When I visited a new internist who came highly recommended, she urged me to visit a neurologist.

"I'd be pleased to have you as a patient but not until you have a firm diagnosis regarding your neurological condition." She referred me to Betty F. Ball, M.D.

In mid-March 1980 I met Dr. Ball for the first time. She took a complete history (I did not at that time mention Marvin Deuring's revelation regarding my MS diagnosis in 1967), and she gave me a thorough neurological examination after which she called me into her private office. There she told me she was quite confident I had multiple sclerosis. A series of diagnostic tests she was ordering would confirm the diagnosis. In a subsequent office visit Dr. Ball told me the tests conducted thus far had confirmed her clinical diagnosis. She arranged to admit me to Barrow Neurological Institute in Phoenix for a two week course of intravenous ACTH treatments. While I was there she would also start me on a regimen of a new antispasmodic medication. She planned to admit me mid-May following her return from a meeting of the National Association of Neurologists.

My stay at Barrow was challenging. For two weeks I experienced incontinence. Lying there in adult diapers I recalled the conversation Dr. Anthony and I had the previous year immediately prior to my misdiagnosis of ALS. I had told him I feared becoming suicidal if I were ever permanently incontinent or had to undergo a colostomy. He nodded sympathetically and acknowledged he fully understood my fear.

Dr. Ball introduced two medications, Lioresal® and intravenous ACTH. The combination appeared to help once I adjusted to some side effects. For the first time since 1963 I could stand flatfooted with my feet together and not fall backwards and to the left. During a lengthy pre-discharge visit Dr. Ball imparted her confirmed diagnosis: MS affecting the spinal cord, brain stem and cerebellum. I suffered from total body spasm, esophageal spasm, perineal spasm, ataxia, diplopia (double vision) and other symptoms too numerous for me to comprehend. Dr. Ball discharged me from the hospital on an extensive medication regimen that included not only the Lioresal but also Dilantin®, imipramine , diazepam, as well as Naprosyn® for arthritis . Dr. Ball also prescribed an electric scooter and authorization for a handicapped license plate for my car . My insurance covered the cost of the scooter and Mother purchased a second hand, wheelchair-accessible van that just happened to appear for sale at a car dealership not five miles from my home. She also covered the $800 cost of equipping it with an electric lift that I could operate easily from both inside and outside the vehicle.

Dr. Ball later shared the ophthalmologist's report. "He states you will be totally blind within the next 12 months." Dr. Ball smiled gently as she imparted this news."

"You're kidding!" I laughed.

Dr. Ball stressed she was totally serious. "You have already lost a considerable amount of your right visual field as well as much of your color sense." Dr. Ball's voice was supportive but left no doubt regarding the facts she was imparting. Her explanation entailed references to rods and cones which were totally beyond my comprehension.

"Well, I decline. That will not happen. I will not be blind."

"How do you plan to avoid it?" Dr. Ball asked.

"I will visualize the myelin recoating my optic nerves and I will pray that God will preserve my sight."

Dr. Ball's concern and skepticism were quite apparent as she slowly shook her head in disagreement. Her eyes were sad, her gaze was penetrating.

"Lynn, given your area of expertise you understand better than an ordinary lay person what denial is all about. Denial may provide short-term benefits but over the long haul, denial will not be your friend."

During my weeks at Barrow's I had experienced both the luxury and the curse of having ample time in which to contemplate my situation. I was 42 years old and no longer able to manage my demanding job with the social service agency I had helped design, fund, develop and manage. I recognized I needed to find less stressful work at a location that did not require a one hour freeway commute each day. In fact, I had recently fallen asleep on the freeway while driving home. Only the bumps demarcating the far extreme express lane had roused me in time to avoid the concrete expressway divider.

In many ways life had seemed less daunting when I thought I was dying from ALS. During those five months visions of life as a severely handicapped person did not stretch endlessly before me as they were now beginning to do. I needed to discover a way to live independently with Multiple Sclerosis. As I lay in bed at Barrow's, my mind kept reviewing scenes from the cruise I'd taken with Mother to the Bahamas the previous summer.

On that cruise with its amazing and highly improbable coincidences, God had placed before my eyes a stark and telling contrast. On one hand there was the courageous Iowa farmwife whose valor in the face of ALS was awe inspiring. On the other hand there was the self-centered MS patient whose moral spinelessness appeared to me to be a far greater handicap than any damage he would ever experience from his MS. I was grateful for the contrast God had shown me. In my heart I knew my only hope of avoiding the self-centeredness and self-pity the man with MS exhibited was to grow ever closer to God and to deepen my faith in Him. I was acutely aware of my tendency toward self focus and self pity. Left to my own devices, I knew I would succumb to both. (Only now as I write these words have I become aware of how judgmental I was regarding the MS patient.)

The God who throughout my life had enabled me to walk again, who had secured a loving caretaker for my children, who then guided me to Arizona where He provided the means for my college education, who gave me the gift of healing from ankylosing spondylitis, who then secured employment for me during my graduate work and paved the path on which I was blessed to benefit many thousands of people through my work with the Foundation for Senior Living—such a loving Heavenly Father would not abandon me. I could place my confidence in Him. My faith in Him had enabled me to walk again despite the grim medical prognosis that I would never do so. My faith in God could preserve my sight if that was His will for me.

Despite my fear and trepidation I knew He would provide all the grace I would require to successfully model myself after the noble Iowa farmwife I'd met on the cruise and who faced the same fatal diagnosis God had then permitted me to avoid. He alone could prevent me from becoming the self-pitying individual on that same cruise who perceived no one's needs other than his own.

Be anxious for nothing, but in everything by prayer and supplication, with thanksgiving, let your requests be made known to God; and the peace of God, which surpasses all understanding, will guard your hearts and minds through Christ Jesus. . . .I can do all things through Christ who strengthens me.

Philippians 4:6-7,13

CHAPTER NINE: FRIENDLY PERSUASION

Mesa, Arizona: 1981-1985

By October 1981 I had exited the non-profit field of social service and entered the profit-making sector of the economy. The printing business I had purchased kept me busy. It was a challenge to learn about an industry that was entirely new to me. My newspaper experience back in the 1950s provided some familiarity with type face and layout. That was essentially my only experience relating even tangentially to the printing industry.

The business I purchased was one which I'd originally been hired to manage. A social worker had sold the business which then landed back in her lap when the new owner's alcoholism resulted in his walking out the door and leaving the press filled with ink and files strewn all over the floor and back office. It took the new pressman and me ten days to reopen the shop and another two days to deal with the long lines of angry customers who had waited more than a month to pick up orders they had placed and had needed. I learned to bid jobs and began to receive orders from printing brokers as well as the local newspaper and various businesses in the Mesa area. I was busy but very lonely.

Then in March 1982 my best friend committed suicide. Dr. Ball had recently diagnosed Sandy as also having MS. Sandy was also rapidly losing her sight. She died in the house I had sold her a year earlier. Sandy was the administrator of the Social Service Department at Maricopa County Hospital. Prior to becoming depressed over her MS diagnosis Sandy had been an extremely gregarious person whose home was frequently the hub for many of us who labored in the social service field or taught at ASU.

Sandy's suicide shocked and saddened all of her many friends. I felt especially bad since I had been the last person to see and speak with her. Both Sandy and I also saw the same psychologist for supportive counseling. Matty did her best to assure me there was nothing I could have said or done to prevent Sandy's suicide. Even so, I regretted the last words I had spoken to Sandy and wished I had never said them.

"Sandy, no one can make you want to live. Only you can make that decision. I urge you to pray about it and to place yourself in God's hands." That Sandy's Bible was open on her bedside table to John 14 afforded a small measure of comfort to me, her family and her other friends.

When I arrived back at my apartment after attending Sandy's memorial service I mourned the world's loss of such a vibrant and witty woman whose organizational skills, work ethic and determination had accomplished so much in the fields of social work both at Maricopa County Hospital and at the Menninger Clinic in Topeka, Kansas where Sandy had worked before moving to Phoenix. I was also deeply angry with Sandy for abandoning us all, especially me. If Sandy—with her previously indomitable spirit—had been unable to face life given an MS diagnosis, then how would I be able to face what lay ahead for me?

I had never felt more desperately alone. My life seemed very small. Could I live on with any degree of satisfaction as a print shop owner—much less support myself with all the expenses an MS patient was likely to incur? Often I slept fully dressed and sitting upright on my sofa because I could not bring myself to lie down and feel totally vulnerable. As an only child whose parents had a bitter and angry relationship, loneliness had been my constant companion. Both as an undergraduate and in graduate school I had always shared an apartment or a home. Now loneliness was my nemesis.

Ashley's rekindled romance in Florida quickly turned to embers. She had returned to Arizona but was living in Phoenix and working in a position for which Sandy had arranged an interview. For the first time in my life—and at the most physically vulnerable time of my life—I struggled to adjust to living alone. I coped by leaving for work at 6:30 AM, eating breakfast at the cafe two doors down from the print shop and then remaining at the shop until 7:30 PM. By the time I dragged myself on crutches from the parking lot to my apartment I was too exhausted to do anything other than eat a few saltines with cream cheese and fall asleep watching TV. While this routine dulled my loneliness, any time I contemplated my future it appeared bleak indeed.

On Halloween afternoon another close friend of Sandy's invited me over to join her and other members of Sandy's "tribe" for a communal meal. There I met a young man named Dan. Dan was new to the Higher Education Department at ASU where our hostess was then an Associate Professor. He and I experienced an instant connection and Dan asked for my phone number which I was glad to provide. A few days later I received a phone call from Deidre (a pseudonym) with whom I had last spoken a dozen years ago when I was an undergraduate. She explained that she and Phoebe (also a pseudonym), another mutual friend, had met Dan for the first time Halloween evening.

"Dan kept talking about the Lynn he had met that afternoon and mentioned she was on crutches. Remembering that you used crutches we asked if this was Lynn Leonard. Dan pulled a scrap of paper out of his pants pocket and your name and phone number were written on it."

The following week Deidre telephoned again to invite me to a Sunday picnic at Papago Park preceded by a tour of the zoo.

"We'll ride the train so that you don't have to walk too far." I accepted the invitation and volunteered to bring a salad. I next heard from Deidre on the Saturday preceding our scheduled Sunday at the park.

"Just wanted you to know we're bringing a new friend along on Sunday so bring enough salad for four."

The weather on Sunday was glorious, just the wonderful weather for which Phoenix is justifiably famous. I had forgotten how beautiful the park was, nestled among Papago's beautiful red buttes. They had always reminded me of Henry Moore's organic, convex sculptures with their pleasing concavities. The almost cerulean blue of the sky set off the buttes' rose colors above which a few white clouds scudded along. It was pleasant to reconnect with Deidre and Phoebe in such a wonderful setting. They introduced me to Mary Wolters and as we strolled through a few exhibits while waiting for the next train to tour the zoo, we exchanged information regarding our respective lives.

I learned Mary was the mother of two adult children and the former wife of a physician who was prominent in the field of substance abuse. When the four of us later accompanied Mary back to her townhouse I discovered some interesting commonalities. Mary had been a Certified Flying Instructor and my son, Steve, was a spotter pilot in Florida. Mary's two sisters lived in Florida and one of the them, June and her husband, Abe, owned a thriving printing company.

Mary then told us about coming home two nights earlier from her work as a Medical Technologist in the Clinical Lab of St. Joseph's Hospital and discovering robbers exiting her townhouse through her second floor master bedroom windows.

"That's the third break-in I've endured in the past year. Both of my cats are terrified and so am I. This time the investigating police officer informed me I'm living in one of the highest crime areas in Phoenix! This really surprised and shocked me."

I could understand why Mary was surprised. She lived in a beautifully landscaped small townhome complex in an area bounded by some of Phoenix's loveliest old homes. Mary had invested in solar panels and in double pane windows to improve her unit's energy efficiency. Thus she was dealing with a definite dilemma: remain living in her considerable investment and risk becoming the victim of additional crime, or relocate and risk losing a great deal of money. Over the following months Mary and I discussed ways to solve her housing dilemma. In the end she rented out her townhouse and together we purchased a three bedroom home in Mesa. It was close to my print shop and also near a freeway which shortened the driving time for Mary's commute. Fortunately her second shift at St. Joe's enabled her to travel the freeway during the hours when traffic was light.

Mary felt much safer in the new home and I was certainly far less lonely. Our schedules provided lots of opportunities for each of us to have the house to ourselves but also enough time together to create a sense of a shared home that was pleasing to us both. During our first two years there we welcomed several family members for both short and extended visits. Mary's sister Ann was our guest on two occasions. My mother visited for a week. My son, Colin, spent several summer months with us and worked with me at the print shop while waiting to return to NC State in Raleigh for the fall semester. Mary's daughter, Kathy, contracted a marriage that was doomed from the start. She separated from her husband the day after Thanksgiving and we returned to Mesa with Kathy and her ten day old son, Stuart, who became the joy of all our lives.

There were also departures during this period. Ashley left on a summer sojourn that evolved into a permanent farewell to Phoenix. She eventually settled in Florida near her dad and his wonderfully nurturing wife, Glenda. Ashley was also near her brother Steve and his son, Zachary. Watching Ashley's departure brought tears to my eyes and left a hole in my heart. Even so, I was grateful Ashley felt she could at last leave the area with the comforting knowledge that I was not alone.

God knew and responded to the depth of my loneliness. He provided a friend whose faith in Him informs her every thought and deed. At a time in my life when I was most vulnerable both physically and emotionally, another of God's serial coincidences connected a man I had met briefly on Halloween with two former friends I had not seen or spoken to in at least 13 years. A few hours later Deidre and Phoebe met Dan, discovered his connection to me and obtained my phone number that he happened to have in his pants pocket. When these two former friends of mine met Mary for the first time only 36 hours prior to the picnic they had arranged in order to reconnect with me, they then invited Mary to join the three of us.

Old friends, new friends—each arranged in an elegant circle by the most loving and faithful Friend of all, just as the old-time hymn proclaims. Mary's cheerful and giving nature are apparent to all who know her. Looking back on the nearly 28 years we have shared a home, I marvel at God's generosity to me. Mary manifests her Christian faith each moment of her life through the loving and consistent support she gives to me and to all who are privileged to know her.

I treasure the two following quotations. Together they describe both the cause and the effects of Friendship.

"Friends are God's way of taking care of us."

Attributed to an anonymous Metro Denver hospice physician

"Friendship doubles our joy and divides   our grief."

A Swedish proverb

CHAPTER TEN:
A SHATTERING EXPERIENCE
Mesa, Arizona: New Year's Day, 1985

On New Year's Day 1985 I experienced another devastating fall. My own pride was in large measure responsible for this fall. In May 1982 I had blithely sold the electric scooter and wheelchair-accessible van I'd used since June 1980. Dr. Ball had voiced her strong disapproval, shaking her head in consternation.

"Whatever possessed you to sell your scooter and van ?" she'd asked.

"Well, if I don't have them then I won't need them. That's my story and I'm sticking to it!" I bantered, only half in jest.

"Lynn, given your profession you should recognize you are in denial and how dangerous that can be," Dr. Ball stated in a grave voice.

I had shrugged off her analysis. I utilized an old pair of arm crutches and, for well over a year ,I managed well without the scooter. It was wonderful to be on my feet again and to look people as much "in the eye" as my 5'1" stature permitted. My New Year's resolution was to regain as much independence as possible. Driving my new Datsun hatchback with its 'Z' engine was exhilarating.

In that spirit I sallied forth to Walgreen's on New Year's Day to pick up some of the numerous medications Dr. Ball had prescribed for me nearly five years earlier. Medications in hand, I headed for the express checkout aisle. Then from beside me I heard a woman's commanding voice.

"John, wait. . ." She ceased shouting mid-sentence as she tripped on my right crutch. The collision knocked me backward onto my bottom. Pain was instantaneous and the most acute I had ever experienced in a life in which pain was neither infrequent nor mild. Simultaneously I felt and heard my fusion shatter. I somehow managed to drive home. For the next ten months I dodged checkups with Dr. Ball and never mentioned my fall to her.

In mid-October when I finally could stand the pain no longer I visited Dr. Anthony who ordered an X-ray. He rushed back into the examining cubicle from viewing the X-ray he had just seen and mounted the film on the viewing panel for me to see. He was clearly agitated. "What happened to your spinal fusion? It isn't there any longer!" Dr. Anthony ordered me to wear a Boston jacket—a one-piece hard plastic jacket that covered the same area of my body as did the body cast I'd worn for six months following my back surgery. However, this time there would be no time limitation. Dr. Anthony informed me I must wear this jacket for 23 hours each day for the rest of my life. Dr. Ball and he conferred by phone and she then called me.

"Lynn, you will never be able to stand, sit or lie down for more than two or three hours at a time." My working days were at an end and once again I was back in an electric scooter, albeit minus a wheelchair- accessible van. At my next visit Dr. Anthony imparted additional discouraging information.

"Lynn, in time you'll discover you are unable to walk at all without the Boston jacket."

In a desperate desire to maintain independence I purchased a rowing machine but just as Dr. Anthony had predicted, it was brutal punishment. The Boston jacket bit into my arm pits and groin. Within two months of seeing Dr. Anthony and hearing Dr. Ball's candid assessment, I sold my printing business and Mary and I then moved to north Phoenix so that Mary could be closer to her job at St. Joe's.

> *For we know that if our earthly*
> *house, this* tent, *is destroyed, we*
> *have a building from God, a house*
> *not made with hands, eternal in*
> *the heavens.*
>
> **2 Corinthians 5:1,7**

CHAPTER ELEVEN:
"BREATHE ON ME BREATH OF GOD"
North Phoenix, Arizona 1986

No sooner had I obtained the Boston jacket in October 1985 than I boarded a plane to Winter Haven, Florida where Mother had suffered her first major stroke. She had occupied her new apartment in a lovely retirement community only a few months when the stroke occurred. Over the following 12 months I made three additional trips to Florida, each journey taxing my physical stamina. By September 1986 I knew I could not physically endure another trip. I located a nursing home in Peoria, Arizona that was minutes from Dr. Ball's office. It was also reasonably near the home Mary and I purchased in north Phoenix after we relocated from Mesa.

For years Mother had begged me to promise that when the time came, I would be there with her so that she would not die alone. I had explained I would do everything possible to be there at that time, but the 2,300 miles that separated us prevented me from being able to promise it would definitely happen. By the time I moved Mother to Arizona in September 1986 she was totally blind and suffering the ravages of chronic infarct dementia. Her brilliant mind was no longer evident. Soon she could no longer complete a sentence. The last coherent sentence Mother spoke was on the day we introduced her to her new room at the nursing home. I was grateful she could not see her surroundings. As pleasant as they were, she would have recognized she was residing in an extended care facility of which she had an intense fear.

"Mother here's your own lovely room!" Mother's response was a question.

"Carolyn, will I. . .will I be able to control my destiny here?"

"Insofar as your Heavenly Father permits!" I replied. This proved to be Mother's last unprompted utterance. During my frequent visits Mother invariably broke my heart by constantly declaring "I want. . ." but without being able to say *what* she wanted. I initially assumed she wanted a cigarette and would ask an aide to wheel her out to the porch up on the roof deck. I would then light a cigarette and place it between Mother's lips, but she seemed unaware of what to do with it. She appeared to have lost the ability to draw on the cigarette. Sadly, I concluded I likely would never discover what Mother really wanted.

On Mother's 78th birthday an aide wheeled Mother up to the roof deck. It was another glorious October day that brought to mind the poem Miss Mary Jackson, my fifth grade teacher, had taught us "October's Bright Blue Weather " by Helen Hunt Jackson. I recited the first stanza for Mother and she appeared to listen and to understand:

O SUNS and skies and clouds of June,
And flowers of June together,
Ye cannot rival for one hour
October's bright blue weather;

It was Mother who had taught me to love poetry and I then began reciting Rudyard Kipling's "L'Envoi." I was delighted when Mother suddenly joined me in reciting the poem she had taught me when I was eight years old:

When Earth's last picture is painted
and the tubes are twisted and dried,
When the oldest colours have faded,
and the youngest critic has died,
We shall rest, and, faith, we shall need it —

lie down for an aeon or two,
Till the Master of All Good Workmen
shall put us to work anew!

And those that were good shall be happy:
they shall sit in a golden chair;
They shall splash at a ten-league canvas
with brushes of comets' hair;
They shall find real saints to draw from
— Magdalene, Peter, and Paul;
They shall work for an age at a sitting and never be tired at all!

And only The Master shall praise us, and
only The Master shall blame;
And no one shall work for money, and
no one shall work for fame,
But each for the joy of the working, and each,
in his separate star,
Shall draw the Thing as he sees It
for the God of Things as They Are!

Rudyard Kipling
L'Envoi to *The Seven Seas* 1898

Mother's voice was clear and strong, as clear and strong as it ever was when I was a child. This proved to be the last time I heard Mother speak aloud and I have treasured that precious memory all these years. For the next three weeks I visited Mother several times a week. On Saturday, November 22, I again visited her. The nursing staff had called to say Mother had begun to refuse food. I thought I could reverse that trend by offering one of her favorites.

"Mother, how would you like it if I made some homemade vegetable beef soup?" Mother turned her face to the wall, bit her bottom lip and said nothing. Suddenly it occurred to me that the next day would be the 45th anniversary of her own mother's death. I became convinced that somehow Mother was aware of that fact and was preparing to reunite with her. The charge nurse informed me Mother was in no immediate danger of dying.

"She could live a long time after eating her last bite."

Unconvinced, when I arrived home I prepared to keep the promise Mother had asked me to make. I would do everything possible to be with her at the time of her death, a death I now firmly believed would occur the following day. The next morning, Sunday, I arose early, dressed and took the Bible from my bedside table with me into the living room. An hour later Mary came downstairs and was surprised to find me up and about—an unusual occurrence following my fall.

"What's up?" she asked.

"Mother will die today." I then explained I was anticipating a call from the nursing home and that barring one, I planned to return to visit Mother in a few hours. Mary looked both dubious and concerned. Half an hour later as we sat reading the Sunday paper and drinking coffee, the phone rang. It was a nurse at the nursing home.

"Mrs. Leonard, I'm calling about your mother. I've been off duty for the past three days and am alarmed by the major changes I see in her. If you want to be with her when she dies, I suggest you come now."

We left for the nursing home immediately where we found Mother lying on her side in the large room in which she was the only occupant. Her breathing was labored but when Mary began reading the 23rd Psalm as I had asked, Mother's breathing eased as I held her hand. I then asked Mary to read all of John 14. As Mary softly read Jesus' words of solace and encouragement and while Mother's breathing grew less audible, I became aware that people I did not know were quietly entering Mother's room.

At first only a few staff members drifted into the room and stood quietly—a respectful distance from Mother's bed where she lay on her side, facing me and with her back to the door. Then as Mary continued to read, I felt a presence that embraced me with an ineffable warmth. I was aware that many more people were silently entering the room as Mary continued to read:

But the Helper, the Holy Spirit,
whom the Father will send in My
name, He will teach you all things
and bring to your remembrance all
things that I said to you. Peace I
leave with you, My peace I give to
you; not as the world gives do I give
to you. Let not your heart be
troubled, neither let it be afraid.

John 14:26-27

Mother drew her last audible breath as Mary read the last verse of John 14. Looking up, I was astonished to see as many as 20 people—strangers to us—who had silently drifted into Mother's room. No words were uttered. Words were not needed. The warm and palpable Presence that embraced us lingered as Mary and I sat with Mother's body for a while longer. I asked one of the nurses who entered the room what she thought had drawn her and all those strangers to Mother's room.

The nurse smiled gently, her face alight. "It was that presence, that warmth. It drew us all."

On our drive home from the care center Mary played a tape of "How Great Thou Art." To this day my memory of Mother's death and the events surrounding it comprise the most ecstatic moments I have ever experienced. In fact, Mother's death eclipsed an earlier death-bed experience that I previously felt could never be surpassed.

☙

I vividly recall the trip that led to that earlier death-bed experience. In August 1974 I had just returned home from an author's workshop. Dr. Kaoru Yamamoto's latest book, *Death in the Life Of Children*, was nearing publication and ten of us had met in a local resort for three days to share our respective chapters with one another. My chapter, "Death in American Life," provided an overview of how we dealt with death in the United States at that time. As I walked in my house the phone was ringing.

Mother was calling to say Dad had lost all kidney function. From the outset of his diagnosis of amyloidosis, Dad had been adamant that he would never agree to dialysis should he loose kidney function. His internist had just told Mother that Dad had perhaps a week to live. I immediately flew home to Florida in order to give Mother emotional support and to say "goodbye" to my father. It seemed a remarkable coincidence to be writing about death at the exact time my father was dying.

When I entered Dad's room he was alert although obviously jaundiced from the disease's damage to his liver. Minutes later Dad's doctor arrived and asked him once again if he would consider dialysis. Dad responded with an emphatic "No." Dr. Mosley then beckoned Mother to follow him out into the hall. As soon as the door closed Dad had begun to shake so violently that his bed's side rails rattled. The look in Dad's eyes was one of intense fear.

"It's scary, isn't it?" I asked in a soft voice. Dad's blue eyes blazed. "What's to be afraid of?" he snapped.

"Well, Dad, it's something you have never done before."

Dad's eyes widened briefly and he immediately ceased shaking. What followed was one of those awkward silences that characterized our time together. I had tried to learn to wait Dad out, to allow him to break these silences. Too often I could not tolerate the silence between us. This time I allowed the silence to continue. It persisted until Mother re-entered the room.

After our brief exchange, Dad lived another eight days and remained remarkably alert up to the end. I was at Dad's bedside with Mother in the early hours of August 23 when my father uttered sounds that had the cadence of speech but were unintelligible to Mother and me. Dad gazed was upwards towards the ceiling and he appeared both elated and astonished.

"Graham, that sounds wonderful! Can you say that again?" Mother asked.

Dad repeated the same sounds in the same cadence while maintaining the same look of ecstasy. And that is how he died just a few moments later. Mother and I independently thought Dad had spoken in Aramaic although neither of us had ever heard that language. At that moment I remember thinking, "Having witnessed Dad's elation at the moment of his death I can never fear death again."

Throughout the years following Dad's death I continued to feel singularly blessed to have witnessed his joyful transition to his new life. I never dreamed that Mother's death 12 years later would also bless me with an experience so profoundly beautiful that it would draw total strangers to her bedside.

Death has been called the last frontier. Mary and I have been so blessed by the ways our parents transitioned to one of the many mansions Jesus promises in John 14. Indeed, Mary's father had just eaten his lunch. His daughter-in-law, Cathy, was clearing lunch trays for Mary's parents from where she had served them in their hospital-styled beds arranged so that they could face one another. These beds stood in front of the home's large picture window and afforded a view of the grass, flowers and trees surrounding the Wolters' Holland, Michigan home. Cathy had turned to place a record of classical music on the hi-fi and her back was to her in-laws when she heard Professor Wolters exclaim, "Look! He's come for me!"

Cathy turned just in time to see Professor Wolters sitting upright in his bed, an expression of joy on his face as he pointed out the window. He then fell back upon his pillow. When Cathy reached his side mere moments later she found he had no pulse.

Today we are learning more about end-of-life experiences. Many physicians have written about their work with patients who have been clinically dead and then revived. These 'near death experiences' among both adults and children afford us opportunities to anticipate what we will experience at the time of death. In reading about what many describe as the White Light—the stunning presence that greets individuals and the life review the dying person then receives from Him—I have no doubt that this is what brought such a look of ecstasy to my father's face and that of Mary's father.

These experiences of our parents' deaths have strengthened our individual and shared bonds of faith. I am grateful Mary was present to share the experience of Mother's last minutes and the palpable, healing presence of the Holy Spirit. Recalling that experience brings to mind one of my favorite hymns, "Breathe on Me Breath of God." The last two verses, shown below, were especially meaningful to me then and they remain so today.

> Breathe on me breath of God
> Blend all my soul with Thine
> Until this earthly part of me
> Glows with Thy fire divine.
> Breathe on me breath of God
> So shall I never die
> But live with Thee the perfect life
> Of Thine eternity.
> Edwin Hatch 1878. Public Domain

Did my mother—plagued by profound dementia—somehow realize the following day would be the anniversary of her mother's death? How did I know Mother would die the next day? The day before Mother's death, the nurse had dismissed my belief. "Your mother can live another two months without eating. She certainly isn't going to die tomorrow."

Was this simply another remarkable coincidence, one of so many that have filled my life? Or did it involve a deeper form of knowledge—a knowing transmitted by the Holy Spirit in a manner I still cannot explain but for which I am immensely grateful? He prompted me to take steps that allowed me to honor my mother's desire that she not die alone. He allowed me to fulfill my pledge to Mother that I would do everything possible to be by her side. The Holy Spirit then embraced each of us present in that room with the warmth of His abiding love. There is no more profound reality than this. He beckons all to draw near. He welcomes all who accept His invitation.

For I am persuaded that
neither death nor life, nor angels

*nor principalities nor powers, nor
things present nor things to come,
nor height nor depth, nor any
other created thing, shall be able to
separate us from the love of God
which is in Christ Jesus our Lord.*

Romans 8:38

Chapter Twelve: Up from the Depths—Again!

Phoenix, Arizona: 1988-2009

While a small inheritance from my mother alleviated my economic challenges, it did not diminish the depression that engulfed me. In addition to constant and severe pain from the shattered fusion and nerve root compression, at age 49 I felt bereft of purpose. During my twenties I had grappled intermittently with major depression. I had struggled throughout my life to overcome a series of physical challenges. During prolonged periods of good health I had felt God had placed me on earth for the purpose of helping others who were physically challenged. Now, once again, I was the one in need of assistance. I seemed unable to help myself much less anyone else. Indeed, the idea of being around other people who needed and used crutches, quad canes, scooters or walkers upset me. Their reality was now my own.

If I am totally honest I confess that I truly felt God had let me down. How much more was I expected to take? "Why me?" was a persistent question that rang in my mind. For nearly two years prior to my mother's death all I had managed to do was move from my bed to our great room where I sat in near-total dejection in front of the television set. One day Mary asked if I would meet with one of her co-workers in the Clinical Lab at St. Joe's. With considerable misgivings regarding what I might have to offer this man, I agreed to meet with him. To my surprise I felt uplifted by our meeting and continued to counsel him on a weekly basis.

A few months later I viewed a *60 Minutes* segment featuring a wheelchair- and ventilator-dependent young man who flew unattended from San Francisco to New York City. Once in NYC he rode the subway alone. I marveled at his courage. Anyone might have yanked loose his air hose. As a quadriplegic he traveled independently. He greeted life on his own terms. In contrast, I cowered cravenly in my living room, too afraid to venture out in public lest another calamity befall me. Yes, I *was* dealing with a calamity—one of my own fear and of its making. I was wasting my life including the abilities God had given me. I began to ask two different questions regarding the physically and emotionally shattering experience that began with that fall in January 1985. Instead of asking "Why me?" I began to ask, "What can I learn?" and also "How can I grow?"

While praying for guidance I remembered Fr. Tom Walsh with whom I had attended graduate school and with whom I had also worked at Catholic Charities. Through the Diocesan Center I tracked him down and we arranged to meet at the Franciscan Renewal Center in Paradise Valley, Arizona. The center is affectionately known as "the Casa," an abbreviation of its Spanish name, *Casa de Paz y Bien.* After listening compassionately to my story Fr. Tom asked how he might help. I knew he had helped establish the Counseling Ministry at the Casa back in the 1970s. I told him I'd like to volunteer as a counselor. He immediately introduced me to Dr. Irene Grier, at that time the director of the Counseling Ministry. Driving home later that day I realized I had agreed to volunteer two days weekly, each day for three hours. I had no idea how I would manage to make the 30 minute commute in each direction and then manage to sit through three consecutive one-hour sessions. However, I was determined to give it my best effort.

My service as a counselor began on January 6, 1988. My first client, *Donna (a pseudonym), was a middle-aged woman whose accent I immediately recognized. At some point during our first session I asked Donna where she was from originally. "Oh, I'm from a little town in South Carolina you have never heard of."

I inquired further and she told me she was from a small town in the Low Country of South Carolina. I did not at that time mention my maternal grandparents' connections to that same small town. I met with this determined woman for the eight sessions the Counseling Ministry allotted annually at that time. When we parted I gave Donna my home phone number should she need to contact me in the future. I hoped our sessions together had helped her to understand that both her painful childhood and her troubled marriage did not reflect upon her worth as a person.

My service at the Franciscan Renewal Center continued during the next two years while I also established a small, private practice as a psychotherapist working from my home. In late September 1989 we moved into a new home where I had a wonderful office in which to counsel clients, both individuals and couples. It was a peaceful setting on the desert preserve. During much of the year from my office my clients and I could hear the sound of rushing water from the waterfall above the koi pond where I spent many enchanted hours observing my beautiful koi, water lilies and the flora and fauna of the desert. My health was steadily improving and I had discontinued use of the Boston jacket. I felt God's healing presence throughout each day, but never more strongly than while counseling at the Casa.

We had moved into our new home on September 29, 1989. The following morning we were in the throes of unpacking when the phone rang. I was amazed to hear the voice of my former client from South Carolina. She wanted to see me immediately, preferably that same today if that was possible. Thus Donna—my first client at the Casa—coincidentally became the first client I saw in my new home office. In the course of that session Donna mentioned a physician who had treated her in the hospital when she was only eight years old. At the end of this session I asked Donna if she recalled that doctor's name.

Donna shook her head. "I'm ashamed to say I don't remember."

When we met for a second session the following week Donna entered my office clutching what appeared to be a framed picture in her arms. "When I got home from our session last week I dragged out an old trunk that has accompanied me in my world travels for the government. Buried on the very bottom of it was this picture and the doctor's name is written on the back."

"Donna, please show me the picture without revealing the doctor's name," I requested. Leaning forward as Donna turned the picture toward me I saw a diminutive, dapper man standing beside a thin little girl who is sitting upright in a hospital bed.

"Donna, I can tell you the name that's written on the back of your picture. That's Dr. Carl Alexander West. He is my grandfather's baby brother." I paused to take a breath before continuing.

"Remember how I've told you that God has a purpose for you?"

Donna nodded slowly, her eyes filling with tears, an expression of wonder on her face. "Yes, and now I'm able to believe that must be true. This is the second time God has used a member of your family to save my life. As you once told me, 'God doesn't make any junk!'" Donna then continued in a whisper that revealed the depth of her wonder.

"Just think about what God has done for me. I've traveled all around the world since that picture was taken of me with Dr. West back in 1948. And more than 40 years later, I connect with a counselor in Phoenix, Arizona which is more than 2,000 miles from my hometown in South Carolina. And the counselor I find—the one I am assigned to meet with—is the great niece of the doctor who saved my life when I almost died 51 years ago."

Donna and I fell silent as we considered how tenderly God had cared for her and was continuing to provide for her. What Donna did not know was how tenderly He had cared for me by prompting me to volunteer at the Casa. God knew precisely what both Donna and I needed and He provided for each of us. My reverie was interrupted by Donna's whispered question.

"Lynn, do you feel it?"

"Yes, Donna. I feel a wonderful, warm presence. I feel I'm being embraced by pure Love." It was a thrill to again experience that same, palpable Presence I first felt not too many months before when my mother lay dying.

Donna's smile was radiant. "Yes, that's it exactly! I feel like I'm receiving a wonderful, warm hug from the Holy Spirit."

After Donna and I completed our work together my health continued to improve during the next nine years. One by one I was able to again discard my scooter, then my crutches and finally my cane. For the first time since 1979 I was able to walk reasonable distances without any mobility aids. I stored these aids in the garage. There I passed them each time I headed out to the car and there, unused, they collected dust—each a silent reminder of God's faithfulness to me.

During those nine years I continued to see clients at the Franciscan Renewal Center two half-days each week. My private practice provided sufficient income to cover many of my expenses with the exception of healthcare insurance. That expense was depleting my inheritance at an unsustainable rate. Even so, I was grateful to be productive. I specialized in working with those who were grieving the loss of physical function or were dealing with other periods of painful transition in their lives, whether death of a loved one or the end of a marriage through divorce. I also enjoyed working with couples who were struggling in their marriages. Life was very good and once again I was grateful God had guided me to the path He wished me to follow in service to others in His name.

Many years after I began volunteering at the Casa I was pleased to be able to invite Gilbert and Kathleen Wrenn to give an in-service training for the volunteer counseling staff, at that time under the leadership of Mauro Pando. It was a truly inspiring few hours during which we listened intently as Dr. Wrenn, then in his nineties and now totally blind, shared with us his wisdom and the depth of his caring for all of God's children who are made in His image. At the end of our training I shared with my colleagues a poem I had written for the Wrenns.

DR. C. GILBERT WRENN

My mentor and friend.

The Greeners

For Gilbert and Kathleen Wrenn

I think of you when I behold
The wonder of a perfect rose.
Wherever I cast my eye today--
Backwards on a quarter century past,
Forward to my nearing years of age,
Inward to the serenity
You seeded in my heart,
Or outwards to others whom
I seek to serve as joyfully
As you have done and do so still,
I find you there—within my core—
The kernel of my best self.

You held and healed me when I hurt;
Guided me when I was lost;
Supported me when I was bereft
Of funds, of health, of strength, of hope.
You never failed me, never criticized.
Through all these years you affirmed
My strength while imparting yours.
Slowly, the tranquility of your life
Transformed the turmoil of my own.

How grateful I am to return to you
Healthy, whole, hope-filled—
Just as you had beckoned me to become.
And blessings beyond measure I discover
You both exactly as I remembered:
Bountiful vessels of God's
Abiding and abundant love.

**1995 Lookout Mountain
Phoenix, Arizona**

Gilbert Wrenn inspired at least two generations of counselors to
follow Dr. Robert H. Schuller's suggestion to, "Find a need and fill
it; find a hurt and heal it." And of course, no one works alone.

*I am the vine, you are the
branches. He who abides in Me, and
I in him, bears much fruit; for without
Me you can do nothing.*

John 15:5

Chapter Thirteen: Trial By Fire

Phoenix: June 5, 1998

On Friday, June 5, 1998 Mary and I had returned to Phoenix earlier in the week from visiting our respective families in Florida. Around 10:00 PM Mary was preparing to go upstairs to her room and was standing at the kitchen sink filling her water glass to take with her. Puzzled by a strange, orange glow in the western sky, Mary decided to check it out from the front door.

"Come quick!" I heard Mary scream. When I arrived at the front door Mary handed me the garden hose.

"Wet down this front wall. I'll call 911 and then wet down the south wall from around back!" Mary commanded as she reentered the house.

The partially constructed home next door was ablaze with flames shooting more than 25 feet skyward. I continued to wet down our house that was only six feet from the nearest wall of the home that was on fire. Soon I realized I was experiencing a burn on my arm and I also recognized the futility of continuing my efforts. Returning to the house I went out back in search of Mary. She was spraying water on the south wall of our house in an effort to prevent it from catching fire. I urged Mary to come back inside. We stood together just inside the back door, each of us praying out loud at the same time.

"Send help, send help." Mary prayed. "Guide and lead us out of here," I prayed.

Our prayers had barely left our lips when there was a knock on our back door. Four teenage boys burst in. "Ladies, you have to come now. Your front windows are beginning to crack!" These young men stripped off their shirts and commanded, "Ladies, cover your faces with these."

One boy picked up Roye, our 14 year old Airedale. Another of our rescuers chased after Mary who was dashing upstairs in search of TyeDye, our geriatric cat. This boy had to drag Mary down the stairs because she had not found TyeDye and didn't want to leave her. With Mary in tow these brave boys herded us around the north side of our house, unlatched the gate that had been stuck and urged us up our steep driveway. I collapsed in our other neighbors' front yard. I tried to persuade the boy who had been helping me to leave me where I was.

"No, you're not safe. You can't stay here. I'll carry you." Even though I probably outweighed him by 30 pounds, this brave young man picked me up and struggled to carry me across our wide street.

"My back and legs are burning!" He screamed.

Yet, despite his pain and fear, he still struggled to carry me across the street to where our neighbors had gathered and the other boys had taken Mary and Roye. My rescuer could have moved far faster without me, but he never set me on my feet so that he could dash to safety. Fortunately, my rescuer's back and legs were not burned. The heat from the intense flames had caused the sensation that his back and legs were on fire.

The story of how these four young men happened to come to our rescue is as remarkable as was their feat of courage. They were friends—three high school seniors and one junior—who had attended a graduation party at a classmate's home. However, they became concerned about the turn the party was taking and decided they should leave. It was early and they didn't want to go home.

"I know a great park near my old grammar school. Let's go hangout there at Lookout Mountain Park" one of the four suggested."

They told us they had been sitting on the swings there in the park fewer than ten minutes when they witnessed the flames shooting skyward.

"We all just started running towards the flames to see if everyone got out okay."

"As we ran up the street we asked a kid if everyone got out of the three houses that were on fire. That kid told us 'Two old ladies live over there in that house but no one's seen them come out.'"

"So we kept running in the direction he'd indicated and we tried to get in through your front door but the trees on both sides of the door were on fire and we couldn't get near because the heat was so intense. That's when we heard the front windows begin cracking. Then we tried to get the gate open there on the north side of your house but it wouldn't open. So we had to scramble up and over the wall that's about six feet tall. We sure were relieved when we dragged you ladies out of the house that we could open your gate at that point! We wondered how on earth we'd get you over the wall if it had still been stuck!"

There were many heroes that dreadful night, all of whom performed courageously to combat the evil deed of an arsonist who had set the fire on the second story of the house next door to us that was under construction. Sixteen pieces of fire equipment combated the fire that destroyed the two homes southeast of us. The Fire Chief came back the following week to survey the desolate scene.

"Ladies, your home came within a minute and a half to two minutes of being totally destroyed."

Despite the $80,000 in damage to our home and a few pieces of furniture, not a single piece inherited from our respective families was destroyed. Miraculously, a fireman found TyeDye while searching for her upstairs in Mary's bedroom where she had hidden under Mary's bed. As he carried Tye's limp and lifeless-looking body across the street to where we sat, we had anticipated the worst. But when he handed her to Mary, Tye managed a pitiful "meow" which was music to our ears. Tye lived another six years and died at the venerable age of 19.

As I recount this terrifying event and its providential conclusion I am awed by the tender care God provided us. Even before Mary and I joined hands to urge God to "Send help! Send help" and "Guide and lead us out of here," His answer to our prayers was already in progress. Four young men followed their sound instincts and left a party that was spiraling out of control. They then made a most unusual decision. They went to a small neighborhood park one of them remembered from his grammar school days. There they chose to sit in facing west, not east. Thus they were looking in the direction of our homes from which they witnessed the precise moment the explosive fire's gigantic flames reached towards the sky.

The distance from the swings on which they sat to the north gate on our side yard is roughly half a mile, a distance these young men covered quickly. Encountering the stuck gate—had they been less agile—they might have taken longer and required more time to vault our wall. According to the Fire Chief, a delay of even two minutes would have been critical to our rescue.

Throughout the 12 years that have followed this fire, Mary and I continue to marvel that our prayers were being answered even before we uttered them. God's graciousness to us continued even following this challenging time. Three different neighbor families asked us to do them a favor by house sitting their homes while they were out of town on lengthy vacations. During the 63 days we could not occupy our home it was not necessary for us to spend a single night in a motel. For just as both of us learned as small children:

> **Are not five sparrows sold for two copper coins?**
> **And not one of them is forgotten before God.**
> **But even the very hairs of your head are all numbered.**
> **Fear not therefore: ye are of more value than many sparrows.**
>
> **Luke 12:6-7**

Chapter Fourteen: My "Fiery" Past
Camden, South Carolina 1923-Tempe, Arizona 1973

In June 1998 fire was no stranger to me. Since early childhood it had been a familiar and disturbing topic in my home. Throughout her life Mother repeatedly recounted the story of the Cleveland School Fire that occurred May 17, 1923 in the small Charlotte Thompson community near Camden, South Carolina.

The Cleveland School sat on property donated by Mother's paternal grandfather, James Franklin West. From my research I have learned this fire was the third school fire on West land. While the earlier fires took no lives, that was not to be the case that May evening in 1923. That night more than 300 people were attending the high school graduation play presented in the auditorium on the school's second floor. When a kerosene lamp dropped onto the stage and engulfed the curtains in flames, many people stampeded the stairs that then collapsed. Because there was but one exit, panic ensued. Finding the stairs collapsed, some people jumped from second-story windows. Many other people plunged to the floor below and were trampled to death by others who desperately attempted to escape through the narrow single door. Soon a pile of bodies blocked the only exit. The fire took the lives of 77 people. Among them were my grandfather's brother Shelton West, his sister Grace West Rhoden, two nieces—Thelma and Rebecca West and one nephew, Jack Rush. The fire's victims were buried in a common grave.

In 1923 my mother was 14 years old. She and her parents had been in Camden just the day before the fire, attending the funeral of Albertus Haile, Mother's only maternal uncle. Mother's two favorite West cousins, Thelma and Rebecca, had pleaded with my grandmother. "Please Aunt Laura, let Martha stay with us so we can all see cousin Jack Rush star in the senior play." But as my mother always explained to me, her mother adamantly refused to leave her in Camden.

My grandmother's explanation had not satisfied her only child. "Martha, I cannot give you a reason you may not stay here with Thelma and Rebecca. All I know is I feel you must come back to Greenville with your father and me." On the countless times my mother repeated this story she always emphasized this important lesson.

"Carolyn, if my mother had not honored her strong feeling despite having no rational explanation for it, I would have been sitting with Thelma and Rebecca and would have burned to death along with them. That means you would never have been born. So Carolyn, you must *always* pay attention to any strong feelings you have. Doing so could save your life or the life of someone else."

☙

The story of my next association with fire occurred more than 50 years later. On December 22, 1973, my parents were to arrive the next day in Tempe, Arizona for a Christmas visit. I was about to undress for bed when my home shook violently shortly before 11:00 PM. At first I thought we were experiencing an earthquake, but then wondered if it were a gas explosion. Looking out the front door of my home I saw a house six doors down the street that was engulfed in flames. Inexplicably, I found myself sprinting barefoot down the street, a feat I had not been able to accomplish in decades.

As I ran I told myself, "Lynn, that's a gas explosion and there could be another one. Turn around! Go back!" My body was unresponsive to this urgent message my brain was sending. Instead, my legs continued to propel me towards the fire. Just as I reached the driveway of the burning house a man and his teenage son crossed the driveway in front of me and entered the front door that had just blown open. The father held a fire extinguisher in his hands. Seconds later I encountered a screaming woman as she stumbled towards me from the carport.

"Get Fred out! Get Fred out!" she begged.

My first thought was one of relief that this woman's neighbors would be the ones rescuing Fred. I did not need to enter a burning house. The woman's hair looked as if she had received a dreadful and nasty-smelling permanent. Then I realized she had been badly burned on her head and face. I took her by the hand and led her next door to her neighbors' home. As we entered the house I saw that her back was hideously burned, totally exposing her entire backside where fire had incinerated her bathrobe.

Once inside I instructed the homeowner to soak clean sheets in the bathtub so we could then wrap the burned woman in them. I thought the wet sheets could help preserve some of her body fluids. Soon a foreign-born neighbor who was a physician but not yet licensed to practice in the United States confirmed the sheets were precisely what were needed. I had already asked someone to telephone 911 for an ambulance.

Workers from the local gas company had been first on the scene followed by the police and then the fire department. The gas company later discovered several of the neighboring houses were full of gas that had leaked from a cracked gas line that had been bent during installation. From a rear window of this home I witnessed a remarkable and puzzling sight. All the dirt in the victim's un-landscaped backyard appeared to be on fire with flames dancing more than a foot high throughout the yard. Her severely damaged kitchen stove sat more than 20 feet into her backyard together with much of the wall that had surrounded it. After attendants loaded this poor woman into an ambulance, her neighbors told me her husband had died just six months earlier.

"Then who was Fred?" I asked just as the father and son I had encountered on the driveway arrived home from battling the blaze next door. The son held a black and white Boston terrier in his arms.

"This is Fred. We found him in the back yard where he landed when the house blew up." Fred, was alive but had lost most of both ears.

When I left the neighbors' house and stepped into the cold December night and inhaled the acrid scent of charred wood, I doubled over with severe stomach cramps. It was several minutes before I could straighten up and begin walking to my home a block away.

Six months later I was shopping for everyday dishes at Diamond's Department Store. A very pleasant women was assisting me in my selection. At some point my attention shifted from the dishes in the display case to the saleswoman's mottled hands, a condition I suspected resulted from serious burns.

"Don't I know you?" the saleswoman asked.

"Do you live near the 3000 block of Evergreen Road in Tempe?" I asked.

Her eyes widened in recognition. "You're the woman who wrapped me in those wet sheets! The doctors in the Burn Unit at Maricopa County Hospital told me those sheets likely saved my life. When I returned home two months later my neighbors and I asked everyone who was there that night if they knew who the woman was who wore a red blouse and plaid slacks. But no one knew who you were or where you had come from. It was like you had come out of nowhere." Catching her breath, she continued.

"When we couldn't discover anything about you—when no one had ever seen you before or since—we jokingly wondered if you were an angel God sent to rescue me.

"You see I suffered third degree burns over 60% of my body. The 4'x4' piece of Plexiglass that covered the "ceiling of light's" six fluorescent tubes melted from the intense heat and then showered straight through my bathrobe, my hair and face and coated those parts of me with hot, melted plastic. Two explosions knocked me down. That second one flattened me after I'd just struggled to my feet. I don't even remember getting up that second time. The next thing I knew I was in the carport and there you were, insisting that I follow you next door."

This dear lady and her neighbors were not the only people who were puzzled by my arrival at her home on December 22, 1973. No one was more amazed than I. For while my health had markedly improved beginning in the spring of 1970, running had not been an activity that I was able to accomplish since the onset of ankylosing spondylitis. On that December night as I sprinted a short block toward the burning house—the same model as my home—my bare feet seemed impervious to the jagged granite landscaping in my front yard and to the rough asphalt pavement on the street.

Why my body was unresponsive to my mind's accurate assessment that the fire resulted from a gas explosion with the likelihood another blast would soon follow, and that I should turn around because I was deathly afraid of fire, is a question that has puzzled me for decades. Everything I know about psychology indicates my deep-seated fear of fire should have triggered a "flight response." It should have directed my steps *away* from a burning house instead of propelling me *towards* the danger I most feared.

My body's total disregard of my profound desire to reverse direction and return home troubled me. It was as if I were having some sort of "out of body" experience in which my brain, my will and my body became disconnected. Why had I put myself in harm's way despite lacking any desire to do so? I did not view myself as engaging in an act of heroism. I wanted to run *from* the fire, not *towards* it.

What could explain my baffling behavior? How did I know to soak the bed sheets to preserve this woman's essential body fluids? The answer to these questions began to reveal themselves more than 25 years after my Christmas-season dash towards that burning house in Tempe, Arizona. I began to comprehend when God sent four young men to rescue Mary and me from the horrendous fire in north Phoenix that threatened our home and in fact, our entire neighborhood. These young men did not live in our neighborhood. Their presence in the park near our home had not been part of their planned graduation celebration. They were sitting on swings in Lookout Mountain Park because they had heeded their God-given instinct to remove themselves from a party that was growing dangerously out of control.

I believe God then prompted these four rescuers to run towards danger just as He had prompted me to run towards danger 25 years earlier. As I write these words I ponder my mother's instructions to me.

"Always follow your instinct!"

However, I claim no credit for following my instinct when I ran towards my neighbor's home in 1973. That night my instinct was God's gift to me and my rational thought did not negate it. Similarly, knowing wet sheets would preserve body fluids was another of God's gifts that long ago night.

There are, I believe, striking and instructive similarities between the mind versus instinct conflict I experienced when I was the rescuer, and the mind versus instinct conflict my personal rescuer experienced as he continued carrying me across a wide street despite believing his back and legs were on fire. The symmetry of these two events centers on the power of God's prompting in our lives and His ability to use His children to overcome danger.

In 1973 the Tempe fire occurred because utility workmen had been too lazy to dig deeper into the desert's rock hard soil. Instead these workers crimped a gas line that eventually cracked and filled three houses with volatile natural gas. In 1998 my neighborhood fire was determined to be the result of arson allegedly the result of a grudge over a money matter. Here malice essentially destroyed two houses, badly damaged a third and easily might have taken lives.

On that December night in 1973 God enabled me to run as swiftly as I had ever run prior to polio and the surgical back issues that followed in its wake. In 1998 four young men were able to scale a six foot high wall with ease— a feat that normally would require military training to accomplish.

How can we account for these eerily similar events? Or of still greater importance, what can we learn from them? I strongly suspect that acts of perceived bravery occur when God's grace manifests itself as an overwhelming instinct that impels a chosen individual to act in ways that are not consistent with his or her human inclination towards self interest. Is it a matter of uncommon courage or an abundance of God's grace whereby He uses ordinary human beings to accomplish angelic feats? As we learn from the words of Jesus found in the Gospels of Matthew, Mark and Luke:

**But Jesus looked to them and said,
"With men this is impossible,
but with God all things are possible."**

Matthew 19:26

Chapter Fifteen:
God's Perfect Timing
Phoenix, Arizona: June 1998-June 2004

In many ways the effects of the arson fire in our neighborhood were fleeting. Mary and I returned to our fully restored home prior to Labor Day, barely three months after the fire destroyed two houses, damaged our home and endangered our lives. Thanks to caring neighbors, we had not spent a single night in a motel. Instead, we "house sat" at three neighboring houses while their owners went on vacation.

Even so, this fire produced long-lasting and profoundly negative effects for me. During the 18 years that preceded this fire I had applauded myself for maintaining the same amount of pain medication I'd received upon discharge from the hospital in June 1980. During these 18 years I had learned to tolerate increasing levels of pain even as my body's tolerance of the mild analgesic diminished its effectiveness. After Dr. Ball Arizona I had relied upon internists for my care and medication management. On the Monday following the fire, I was stunned when the internist I'd seen during the preceding year recommended a change in medication.

"Lynn, I believe you have been under-medicated for pain for many years. I'm also concerned that the medication you've used for nearly two decades could adversely affect your liver. That medication is not intended for long-term use, especially in such large doses. There are some new medications on the market but I suspect they may well produce side-effects. In contrast, morphine has been around for a very long time. It's main side-effects are addiction and constipation. You don't have an addictive personality and there are ways to manage the constipation.

"You will require more and more morphine over time, but that won't be a problem. Don't worry about it!" she continued.

By June 2004—six years later—I was extremely discouraged. I no longer recognized myself or my life. Just as the internist had predicted, my daily consumption of extended-release morphine had steadily increased. I was now taking 200 mg daily plus an additional 30 mg of fast-acting morphine for "break-through" pain. I abhorred being dependent on such heavy-duty narcotics. It diminished my short-term memory, but what concerned me far more was the heavy burden it placed on Mary's shoulders. For it was Mary who had to make my monthly "drug runs" to the doctor's office to pick up my prescription, and it was Mary who then had to drive to the pharmacy to have them fill the prescription. The future looked grim as I contemplated the continuation of this monthly regimen for the rest of my life, or Mary's.

Nor was this my only concern. On an almost daily basis newspapers and television carried horror stories about the ease of addiction from various forms of these morphine-based medications. The media reported innumerable robberies tied to youths who were addicted to this drug. The media also frequently reported on deaths from accidental overdoses. I feared I might go to sleep some night and not awaken in the morning. Each night I prayed for release from pain and release from my dependency on this drug. Each morning I thanked God for bringing me safely through another night.

This is where things stood with me in June 2004 when I received an email from a friend, Carol Pletz, suggesting I check out a fruit called *mangosteen* online at the National Library of Medicine's website. I was intrigued yet extremely skeptical. The early research appeared promising and I was especially impressed with a lengthy report detailing the anti-inflammatory properties of a few specific properties (xanthones) within this mangosteen fruit, *garcinia mangostana*.

However, in speaking with Carol Pletz I learned the company offering this juice product was both a start-up and a network marketing company. This news concerned me. I had already experienced three major disappointments in network marketing—even though my business partner and I had prayed prior to participating in them. Disappointment when these ventures failed was still fresh in my mind. After these three disappointments, Mary and I had long ago concluded we had somehow misunderstood God's intention for us with respect to network marketing. My response to Carol was firm and unequivocal.

"Thanks, but no thanks! We're no longer interested in anything to do with network marketing."

And yet, I did find the research I had reviewed to be intriguing. What if this new product might help with my pain and thereby help reduce my dependence on morphine? Each night I continued to pray that my pain would lessen and to be freed from morphine. Each morning I thanked God for allowing me to awaken.

Two weeks later when Carol called she spoke with Mary and invited us to attend a presentation on this juice. Mary thought we should attend and we went to a presentation by a physician, a pharmacist and Sandi, the pharmacist's wife. Sandi was no stranger to pain. For 23 years no medication had controlled—much less eliminated her migraine headache pain—pain that put her to bed in a darkened room as many as seven or eight days each month. Since drinking this juice regularly, migraines no longer interfered with Sandi's life. Sandi's story grabbed my attention.

What most impressed Mary as a Medical Technologist was how this juice's xanthones appeared to have reduced Sandi's C-Reactive Protein (CRP) marker. It fell from an elevated 8.9 down to 0.9, a normal reading. Hearing this, Mary became more open-minded about the product's efficacy. Mary helped me understand that the CRP is a marker of inflammation. Mary also explained that inflammation is a contributing factor in many, if not most, diseases. That night I decided to see if the juice might help with my pain just as it had helped with Sandi's. My goal was to reduce the amount of morphine I was taking each day—not only the rapid-acting morphine I took for break-through pain—but also the extended-release morphine. Within ten days Mary noticed I was less hunched over from muscle spasm and spasticity. I realized I wasn't reaching as frequently for the break-through pain medication. Within two weeks I had completely eliminated the use of the break-through medication—a daily reduction of 30 mg of morphine. Prayerfully, over the next few months, I was able to *totally eliminate all narcotic and analgesic medication.* I had regained my life!

When some of my other physical symptoms also improved, I was surprised and delighted. The gastric reflux that had plagued me for 20 years totally abated. Also, I was no longer troubled by the urinary incontinence that had begun with that major MS exacerbation in 1980 and had since worsened progressively. My blood pressure plummeted from a high of 158/95 down to 117/65. This new reading was *without* blood pressure medication and in fact was much lower than at any point during the three years I'd been taking medication to lower it. Friends and neighbors could hardly believe their eyes when they saw the difference in me. Before long, several friends and neighbors were also ordering the juice. God had heard and answered my prayers. A delicious juice made from an ugly, little purple fruit from Southeast Asia was reducing my pain!

For the past six years I have celebrated June 29 as my "Rebirth Day." That is the day on which my adventure with this God-inspired product began. My gratitude to Carol for introducing me to this juice is boundless. I cannot adequately convey my gratitude to God for creating this fruit and to the men who risked everything they had to bring this product to market. I am also grateful that Mary and I did not permit our earlier negative experiences in network marketing to turn us away from this product and this company.

There have been many remarkable "God winks" regarding our association with this juice. One of the earliest of these coincidences occurred when we were leaving Salt Lake City after attending our second company convention. We were in an airport shuttle and feeling tired but at the same time exhilarated about all we had learned from distributors around the globe as well as from the inspiring presentations of the company's six founders. In the shuttle Mary and I fell silent as we pondered all of this. Then I happened to recognize a familiar accent as the couple seated in front of us chatted about the convention.

"Pardon me, but are you folks from South Carolina?" I inquired. The reply was prompt.

"Yes, we're from Hilton Head."

"By any chance do you know John Carl West, the former governor, who also lives in Hilton Head?"

The woman in front turned to face me. "I should say I do know John West. I was his secretary for many years!"

Shown above: Future SC governor John Carl West in the arms of his father, Shelton West. Photo was taken just 25 days prior to the Cleveland School fire near Camden, SC that left little John and his older brother Shell Jr., (shown on left) fatherless. (Description of this fire begins on page 192.)

Several other striking events have occurred during the past six years that have strengthened our confidence that we are on the path God wishes us to follow. The first event occurred in our second year when the author Richard Paul Evans spoke to a group of distributors in Phoenix. In the course of his presentation he mentioned he had just that night flown in from Florida where he had met with programs addressing the issue of spouse abuse. When I approached him after the meeting I introduced myself and mentioned that my daughter had served for many years as the executive director of Hope Family Services in Bradenton, Florida. Mr. Evans' face lit up. "I spoke there last night at their fundraiser!"

Then in May 2007 I was packing to attend the company's regional conference in Las Vegas. I was in my closet trying to reach something on a shelf above my head when a small Kodak album of photos landed on the floor at my feet. Picking up the album I thumbed through the pictures and recognized them as having been taken in 1952 at a Tri Zeta slumber party held at my home in Greenville, South Carolina. Tri Zeta was a new "sorority" that my mother and the mother of some other girls had organized when their daughters had not been chosen as members of the other three junior high clubs that were the hub of all the social life for Greenville's sub-debutante crowd. I showed the pictures to Mary and resumed packing for Las Vegas.

In Las Vegas, Carol and John had rented a condo for members of their organization, many of whom were not from the Phoenix area. On my second evening with this group I sat next to Jackie, a striking and delightful woman whom I did not know who was attending the regional with her wonderful son, Hank. As Jackie and I chatted I recognized a familiar accent.

"Jackie, where are you from originally?"

Jackie replied she was from Greenville, South Carolina and of course, I said that was my home as well. Further conversation revealed that Jackie was two years younger than I and thus two grades behind me in school.

"My parents and I attended Buncombe Street Methodist Church," Jackie volunteered.

"So did my parents and I!" I exclaimed.

Jackie and I were relishing these connections when Jackie asked, "Were you a member of any of the little social clubs there at Greenville Junior High? I was a member of Tri Zeta."

Smiling, I told Jackie how I came to be among the group who founded Tri Zeta. "My mother and a number of other mothers formed Tri Zeta so we would not miss out socially. The mothers had things all planned out. I was to be the first president but I foiled that plan when I refused to vote for myself. I thus became Tri Zeta's first ever vice-president instead."

In her excitement Jackie pounded the arm of her chair. "Lynn, my mother told me that story shortly before she died! She said, 'Jackie, there was this girl who could have been the first president of Tri Zeta but she didn't vote for herself. Now Jackie, remember you must *always* vote for yourself!'"

Jackie and I sat absorbing the improbability of this entire scenario. Then, when I told Jackie about the Kodak photo album that had fallen from a shelf in my closet and landed at my feet as I was packing to come to Las Vegas, the improbability of it all increased exponentially. Out of 5000 distributors attending that regional conference, Jackie and I were sharing a condo because the son who sponsored her had been sponsored by Carol Pletz who *coincidentally* had also sponsored Mary and me.

TRI ZETA'S FIRST PAJAMA PARTY

Above: This 1952 picture coincidentally fell at the author's feet as she packed for the Las Vegas 2007 Regional. Author appears back row, center, and is "vertically challenged." Jackie is not in this photograph because she did not join Tri Zeta until 1953.

TRI ZETA SISTERS' REUNION

Above in Front Row, L-R: Tri Zeta sisters Jackie Neaville and author. Back row: Carole Rajkovski and Carol Pletz. XanGo 2007 Regional in Las Vegas. Photo courtesy of Carol Pletz.

Once again improbable events occurred that I perceived as indicators I was on the right path. And as our business has grown, Mary and I have come to realize that had we not been involved with each of those failed network marketing ventures, we would never have met Carol and John Pletz. I likely would still be taking massive amounts of morphine or perhaps dead from an accidental overdose. And without our previous experience in network marketing and the lessons learned from them, we would not be where we are today.

My introduction to this product and this company came as a direct answer to prayer. In both 1995 and 1998 we had prayed regarding network marketing, asking guidance regarding our involvement in this industry. Then from June 1998 until June 2004 I had prayed to be relieved of my dependence on morphine. God answered both prayers and has now blessed me with restored health that does not require reliance upon narcotics or other analgesic medications, provided I am faithful and consistent in drinking my favorite juice.

Perhaps of even greater importance, we have been privileged to bless the lives of many others by sharing news of this product and the company that developed it. Here is but one example of such shared blessings. This story involves another remarkable example of God's coincidental guidance. In fact I believe it is possibly the most striking story of such guidance among the many I have experienced throughout my life.

In November 2007 our former neighbor, Darrell Mankoff, telephoned me from his amazing art gallery in Scottsdale, *Work of Artists*.

"Lynn, expect a call from one of my finest artists, Kathy Bechamp. Her brother came by today to tell me Kathy has some dreadful form of thyroid cancer. So I sent two bottles of juice home to her along with your phone number. I'll call her today to make certain she checks in with you."

When Kathy telephoned me the following day we spoke for a long time. I had never heard of anaplastic thyroid cancer (ATC) and asked Kathy about her prognosis. There was a long silence.

"Well, they tell me if I do all the radiation and the chemo this clinical trial back in Virginia calls for, that I then could live another two or three months."

Kathy's grim prognosis shocked and saddened me. Here she was, a talented 54 year old artist who had established a school for children in central America and whose fiancé had died of cancer six years earlier. Now her doctors were telling her she would not live longer than three months no matter what she did.

We spoke for a while longer and Kathy asked, "How much of this juice should I take?"

"Kathy, let me contact Dr. Amod Tootla and ask him what he would recommend for you. He is a world-renowned cancer specialist and even though he works with colorectal patients, he has had more clinical experience using our product as a supplement with cancer patients than anyone I know. I'll get back with you as soon as I've heard from him."

After saying "goodbye" I began sorting through my disorganized desk in search of Dr. Tootla's phone number. Only moments later the phone rang and when I answered, I heard a distinctive voice that revealed Dr. Tootla's childhood years spent in South Africa and the influence of his parents who were natives of India.

"Is this Lynn Leonard? This is Dr. Amod Tootla calling from Michigan about the letter you sent me a year ago regarding a physician's interest in using the juice with pediatric burn patients. I fear your letter has been buried on my desk for all this time. I do apologize."

Shaking off my amazement I replied, "Dr. Tootla, I was searching for your phone number buried somewhere on *my* desk when I answered the phone and here you are! I'm afraid that doc has moved on, but I really need your help with a young woman who phoned me just a few minutes ago." After listening to my description of Kathy's condition, Dr. Tootla advised that Kathy should drink a bottle of juice each day for a month followed by three quarters of a bottle daily during the second month.

"And how much should Kathy drink in the third month?" I asked.

Following a rather lengthy pause Dr. Tootla replied, "Lynn, there likely won't be a third month. Anaplastic thyroid cancer is universally and rapidly fatal. All she can do is try the juice to see what it might do for her." After promising to keep Dr. Tootla informed of Kathy's progress and asking her to forward to him her lab reports and records regarding her chemo and radiation protocols, I telephoned Kathy.

"Wow, that was fast!" Kathy exclaimed when I told her I had just spoken with Dr. Tootla. I described how, following my conversation with her, I had just placed the phone back on its cradle and was searching for Dr. Tootla's phone number when the phone rang and I recognized his voice, distinctive because he is from South Africa and his parents were from India.

Kathy continued, "Lynn, this is like a miracle, isn't it? What are the chances that this world famous doctor would telephone you right after you and I had spoken for the first time and just at the very moment you were searching for his phone number? This gives me more hope than I've had in months. I know I'm being guided to try this juice."

After letting her radiation oncologist know her plan to try the juice, Kathy consumed a bottle of juice each day for the next month. When her throat closed from a radiation stricture, with her doctor's approval Kathy placed the juice in her feeding tube with her homecare nurse's assistance. Kathy continued consuming large quantities of juice through her feeding tube and, by late March, Kathy was declared "cancer free."

In April Kathy attended her first chemo support group after which she phoned me. "Lynn, all these people were complaining about nausea and sharing their horror stories. I told the group I never experienced any nausea and they couldn't believe it. Some of them also had undergone radiation and talked about their extreme fatigue. I told them I had lots of energy and that I had just driven roundtrip to California to display several of my quarter-inch steel pieces in an outdoor gallery there. I explained I believe the juice kept my energy level up while also preventing my nausea."

In July when Kathy's lung collapsed following a failed surgical attempt to remove the radiation stricture that had closed her throat, she phoned and asked us to bring some juice to the hospital. We told her that her doctors and the hospital likely would not allow her to take the juice while a patient in Intensive Care.

"Guys, my docs are so impressed with my lab work that they have no issues with me taking the juice. Just come to the door of the ICU, hold up the bottle and the nurse will let you in." And that is what we did. The ICU nurse escorted us to Kathy's bedside and watched as Kathy poured the juice directly into her abdominal feeding tube.

While it was remarkable that Kathy never experienced any nausea from her chemotherapy and no fatigue, these were not the most striking outcomes of adding the juice to her treatment regimen. In the clinical trial in Virginia there were seven other people who underwent the same chemo and radiation protocols as Kathy's. Sadly, all of them died within a twelve-week period, just as Kathy's oncologists had predicted would be her fate. Of these eight patients, Kathy was the only survivor.

The months rolled by and Kathy soldiered on—her only source of sustenance provided by several cans daily of liquid nutrition and our juice. She searched for surgeons who had sufficient experience to successfully repair her throat so that she could once again could eat and swallow. As more time passed Kathy grew increasingly discouraged that her only nutrition came through a feeding tube. However, there was also good news. She had located a surgeon in New York City who was eager to repair her throat. He had successfully repaired the throats of many others whose conditions were similar to Kathy's. When Kathy and I spoke at the end of June 2009 Kathy told me she had once again been deemed "cancer free." However, I heard a weariness in Kathy's voice I had never heard before.

"Lynn, I'm down to the final appeal with my insurance company. If their decision is final and they don't provide coverage for the doc in NYC to repair my throat, then I'm at the end of the road." I thought back to what Kathy had told me the first time we had spoken in October 2007.

"Lynn, I have to decide if I even want to submit to all the radiation and chemo. Even if that gets rid of the cancer, my quality of life will be dreadful if I wind up unable to eat and swallow. I wouldn't want to live like that."

Kathy remained cancer free until early July 2009 when her insurer declined her appeal to cover surgery by the NYC specialist with such success in removing radiation strictures such as hers. Upon learning her throat would not be repaired, Kathy stopped taking the juice. Later in July she developed a high fever and was hospitalized. A biopsy revealed anaplastic cancer cells in her kidney. Kathy died on October 21, 2009 after a valiant battle of almost 24 months against a rare cancer known for its rapid progression and universal lethality. Kathy had exceeded her projected life span by 21 months. And throughout her rigorous chemo and radiation treatments Kathy had experienced no nausea and no crushing fatigue.

What have I concluded from these particular coincidences? Due to our nation's prevailing culture I believe many, if not most of us, expect rapid responses—whether from the medication or supplements we take, in career advancement, in securing our financial futures or even in response to our prayers. Our culture has also grown increasingly less comfortable with uncertainty or ambiguity. Many of us expect and are comfortable only with clarity and with what appears to be a "sure thing." Therefore, it is not the least surprising that we often expect God to answer our prayers with either an immediate, unambiguous "Yes" or "No." We neither anticipate nor welcome a less emphatic response such as "Not yet!" or "Wait!"

With the understanding that only hindsight's 20/20 perspective can provide, I now recognize that God's "Not yet" or "Wait" can be not only a time of frustration for the petitioner, but also one of preparation and personal development. For example, we now realize that having prayerfully participated in three networking companies that failed, Mary and I did not come away from those disappointing experiences empty handed. We gained valuable training and personal development skills that have benefited us immeasurably.

Of even greater importance—from a faith perspective that my personal experience strongly validates—I know our Heavenly Father is not a trickster. When we pray for His guidance in our lives, He guides us upon a certain path. Our journey may be challenging as was that of the Israelites during their 40 year sojourn in the desert. Yet God gives us signs to follow just as He guided His chosen people with a cloud by day and a fire at night and by the Ark containing His Holy Word. Therefore, let us pray without ceasing and move forward boldly with faith, acknowledging with gratitude the signs— the coincidences—by which God provides guidance to us for our personal life journey.

∞

Had Mary and I allowed discouragement about those three early disappointments in network marketing to stand in our way, we would not have learned about the product that turned my life around. I quite likely would not have survived continued use of such large daily amounts of extended-release morphine and Kathy Bechamp likely would have died nearly two years earlier than she did. In addition, throughout the past six years I have been privileged to speak with countless people who have friends or relatives who are experiencing health challenges.

While I freely acknowledge that not everyone will experience the remarkable blessings both Kathy and I enjoyed as a result of drinking this delicious juice, my heart overflows with gratitude that God strengthened our faith in His will and that He is allowing us to bless so many people by sharing the opportunity this company offers to improve both the physical and financial wellbeing of others. Daily I pray that God will guide me to those who need the physical and/or financial blessings our company and its products can offer them. I feel blessed to be a blessing.

God opens doors and points us on the path He would have us follow. But He will neither force us through those doors nor drag us down those paths. Once we have prayed for guidance and have felt we received a clear indication of God's will, we must not succumb to doubt or wallow in despair if the results are not immediately what we had anticipated. Trust in the Lord, that His will for you may become manifest. And trusting, then heed the wisdom of St. Augustine of Hippo who instructed, "Pray as though it all depends on God and work as though it all depends on you!" God has in mind for His family only that which is good.

For I know the thoughts that I think toward you, says the Lord, thoughts of peace and not of evil, to give you a future and a hope.

Jeremiah 29:11

Chapter Sixteen: On Eagle's Wings

From Florida & Maryland to the Grand Canyon: 2009

Visits with family members filled us with joy throughout the spring and summer of 2009. The week of Memorial Day Mary's son David was on leave from duty as a Navy physician and visited us with two of his three daughters and his new granddaughter, Kaylee. Only days later, my daughter Ashley was in town for the second straight year, this time for a conference. We made plans to vacation in Michigan with Mary's siblings, cousins and also her grandson, Stuart, who had just completed his second year at Garrett Evangelical Seminary where he was working on his Master of Divinity degree. While we were finalizing those plans, my former daughter-in-law, Cindy, returned to Phoenix in July for the second time in five months. This time my grandson, Jacob Glenn Leonard, came along. I was thrilled and we hurriedly made plans to show Jake as much of Arizona as possible during the week he would be with us.

The Grand Canyon is deservedly one of the most visited tourist sites in the world. Its majesty is, in my opinion and that of most visitors, without parallel. Given such short notice I had little hope of securing tickets on the Grand Canyon Railroad for the trip to and from the Canyon via Williams, Arizona. I also thought Jacob would find Kartchner Caverns south of Tucson to be of interest. Which tour, if either, we could reserve was the question. I contacted AAA to make arrangements, saying a prayer that Jacob would be able to see at least one of these natural wonders. I was thrilled when the dates I had requested for both the Grand Canyon and Kartchner Caverns were available.

The morning after Jacob's arrival we left home early in the morning for the trip by car up to Williams, Arizona where we would stay at the Grand Canyon Railway Depot Hotel and then board the train the following morning for the ride to the Canyon. We stopped in Sedona for a leisurely lunch and Jake loved the beauty of Sedona's famous red rocks. We arrived in Williams in late afternoon, checked into our suite and enjoyed the buffet dinner at the lodge.

After breakfast the next morning we boarded the train and arrived at the Canyon dining room where we had reservations for lunch and from which we would then board a bus for the tour of the Grand Canyon. A pleasant young woman volunteered to carry my tray and guided me to a table in a far corner that was designated for the handicapped. Mary and Jacob and I had been seated only a few minutes when I sensed someone standing beside me.

"May we join you?"

Glancing up I saw a tall, slender and attractive woman whom I judged to be about Ashley's age. With her was a very tall young man who looked to be a few years older than Jacob. The five of us introduced ourselves and exchanged a few pleasantries and before long, we heard the announcement that we all needed to board the buses for the Canyon tour. Our table guests departed after we said goodbye thus ending our brief and pleasant encounter.

Jacob was in awe of the Grand Canyon as were Mary and I. I recalled my first glimpse of it during the trip Jacob's granddad and I had made with my parents following my high school graduation in 1956. Despite having been at that time three years older than Jacob, I somehow had failed to appreciate the Grand Canyon's beauty and vastness. In marked contrast, Jacob declared it was far more impressive than he had anticipated.

We had been taking numerous pictures when our path crossed that of our lunchtime table companions to whom we nodded without engaging in lengthy conversation. Everyone was busy taking photos.

Jacob was especially pleased to catch a shot of a California Condor and another of an American bald eagle. Much too soon we again boarded our bus and found ourselves back at the depot where we waited to catch the train back down the mountain to Williams.

To my surprise we also encountered our table companions at the depot. This time we had a chance to chat at length. Mary and I learned that Sue Goldsmith and her son, Patrick, were on vacation from Maryland. Patrick was hoping to enter the military. Mother and son were also planning a two-week trip into Utah's Bryce Canyon and Zion National Park and then on into Wyoming to the Grand Tetons and Yellowstone. We urged them to include Sedona in their itinerary even if it meant backtracking to do so.

At some point Sue mentioned a back condition that caused her considerable pain. I shared with her that I, too, had back problems. We exchanged contact information before Mary, Jake and I boarded the train back to Williams. Two weeks later I emailed Sue and thus began an amazing adventure. Through emails we discovered that Sue's mother and grandmother were from my home town in South Carolina. I also shared with Sue how much the juice had helped me with my back and muscle pain. Many weeks later, Sue laughed.

"Do I have to beg you for this juice?" I was delighted when Sue phoned me just a few days after receiving her shipment. Sue continued, "I can't believe how much it is helping me! I've already been able to reduce my pain medication and muscle relaxants."

In January 2010 we invited Sue to visit us in Phoenix and to our delight, she accepted our invitation. After visiting us, Sue then flew to Salt Lake City. There she rented a car and drove to Lehi where she toured the company's corporate offices prior to two days of skiing before returning home to Maryland. Sue was delighted with the reception she received at corporate where she met with two of our company's founders, the C.E.O. and the senior vice-president for product development.

SUE GOLDSMITH IN UTAH

Sue Goldsmith (center) visits XanGo Corporate Offices.

L-R: Founder Joe Morton, President and CEO Robert Conlee, Sue Goldsmith, Founder Gordon Morton and Senior Vice President Beverly Hollister. Photo courtesy of Sue Goldsmith.

"Those people are amazing. I was brand a new independent representative with the company and they treated me like a queen!" (This tour was graciously arranged by Carolyn Johnson who, together with her son Tommy and daughter Cathy Kalos—a stay-at-home mother of four sons—have built large international businesses in the very family-friendly arena of network marketing.)

Then in late April 2010 Sue joined me at the company's regional meeting in Las Vegas after which she returned with me to Phoenix. One night as Mary, Sue and I lingered over dessert, Sue revisited the improbable way in which we had met.

"You know, I remember feeling drawn to where you three were sitting way off in that corner of the dining room there at the Grand Canyon. And then Patrick and I bumped into you guys on two more occasions. The first time we were all caught up in looking at the Grand Canyon and so we just greeted one another in passing. But that third encounter was such a remarkable happenstance. Patrick and I were just strolling around taking pictures of a California condor we'd been following. We had no intention of going to the Depot—in fact we had no reason to do so. But when I looked up from tracking that condor, there you three were again and so we had more time to chat.

"And it was there at the depot that I mentioned my back pain, something I don't usually share with people, especially with someone I've just met. And then at the end of our conversation you said, 'Sue, if you ever return to Phoenix, please plan to stay with us.' When you saw how surprised I was by your invitation, you said. 'I've never invited someone I've just met to stay at our home, but for some reason I'm totally comfortable inviting you.' Then, months later in one of our phone conversations, you confessed you'd actually been surprised when you heard yourself invite me to stay with you and Mary.

"And now I've come to visit the two of you not just once, but twice. I am convinced this is part of God's plan for my life. I don't know where this is going to end up but I'm on board for the ride!"

In April 2010 on her last night with us before returning to Maryland, Sue told us how she came to be at the Grand Canyon on that particular tour.

"When I called AAA to make our reservations at the Grand Canyon, the woman told me she'd do her best but thought it unlikely she'd be able to make reservations for the days I wanted. So when she called back to say our reservations were exactly as I had requested, I was quite surprised."

Hearing this, Mary and I smiled at one another. "Sue, we also used AAA for reservations and were told the same thing. In fact, I had given them two different dates. I told the woman at AAA that we'd prefer to do the Grand Canyon tour on the earlier date if at all possible and to tour Kartchner Caverns four days later. Like you, Mary and I were warned the date we wanted for the Canyon tour might not be possible and we were both surprised and delighted when the date we preferred for viewing the Grand Canyon was available.

Sue, Mary and I were silent for a few moments as we contemplated again the marvelous way God had arranged our encounter.

"This was no accident, no mere coincidence!" Sue proclaimed and Mary and I concurred.

God had arranged for us to meet on three separate occasions when our lives intersected during those few brief hours at the Grand Canyon. In fact, it appears that God used one of his amazing creatures, a California condor, to connect Sue, Mary and me for that fateful third encounter during which I extended the invitation that has now brought Sue on two visits to our Phoenix home.

Sue says she has always felt the Southwest is where she is meant to live. "There have just been far too many "happenstances" for me to ignore. At first I was simply grateful to find two ladies who might fill the void left by the death of my mother and mother-in-law just months before I met you two. Now I truly believe God is pointing my path towards Phoenix and towards the opportunity to help others maintain or improve both their physical and their financial wellbeing."

As I write about Sue's affinity for the Southwest a vivid memory comes to mind. I see myself as a little girl of three or four. My long hair moves rhythmically as I ride back and forth on my rocking horse on the large front porch of my home in Greenville. I'm singing a song my mother taught me, "Ragtime Cowboy Joe," who lived "out in Arizona" or "Don't Fence Me In" about "riding to the ridge where the West commences. . . ." Growing up in an era when children went to the movies every Saturday morning to see Westerns I became quite familiar with landscapes in which saguaro cactus was as much a signature as Tom Mix, Gene Autry or other famous western stars from that era.

As a practitioner of cognitive behavioral therapy I firmly believe our words inform our hearts and minds. During the 46 years I've lived in Arizona—despite having felt driven here by health issues and forced to live far apart from family and friends—I truly believe the countless hours I spent rocking on my hobby horse in early childhood prepared my heart and mind to be as content as possible out in Arizona with its wide open spaces and stately saguaros. I made a home on the range where, indeed, "the skies are not cloudy all day." And that was precisely what my orthopedists in North Carolina recommended and likely also has helped keep my depression bay.

⊗

In the fall of 2009 I heard from *Shelly a former client with whom I worked some 15 years earlier. I was delighted to hear from this exceptionally bright and accomplished woman who had enjoyed a successful career as in an allied health field. Due to her own health challenges she subsequently left her chosen field and became equally successful in a premier network marketing company that like mine is also headquartered in Utah. Shelly explained she was calling to make a referral of one of her distributors, a woman I shall call *Kristen. Even though I am retired and seldom see new clients for counseling, I agreed to see Kristen. Kristen and I were concluding our second session when her Southern accent registered with me.

At first she stated she was from High Point, North Carolina but when I mentioned that my grandmother, father and former husband were all from the nearby town of Thomasville, Kristen's eyes sparkled.

"Really!" she exclaimed. "That's actually where I was raised."

Kristen and I discovered numerous additional connections. Her mother had adored my dear friend and former mother-in-law, Hazel Leonard. Kristen stated that her mom loved to send flowers. "Mom probably stopped by Elliott's Florist on a weekly basis. She told me that speaking with Hazel Leonard just made her day!"

At some point Southern cooking came up and Kristen mentioned that her aunt was famous for her coconut cake. I mentioned that my father-in-law, who had been a Jewel Tea salesman, every week or so brought home to all of the family the most delicious coconut cake I had ever eaten. At Christmas, when Kristen went home, she asked her 84 year old aunt if she remembered a Jewel Tea salesman who used to buy cakes from her.

"Yes, that was Paul Leonard and he adored my coconut cake."

---

*   Shelly and Kristen are pseudonyms

These "coincidences" were very reassuring to Kristen. "I think these coincidences tell me I've found the right therapist!"

Over the ensuing months additional coincidences surfaced that served to further strengthen Kristen's conviction that she was precisely where she needed to be. As a therapist I have encouraged clients to strive for a balanced life. That includes finding some area in which they can enjoy serving as a volunteer. And so I asked Kristen if she had any interest in horses and children.

"I love them both. Why do you ask?"

"Well, I know of a therapeutic riding program to which I've occasionally referred several clients. One of them had never even ridden before. She learned to ride and later became one of their instructors."

Kristen's eyes sparkled. "I guess the next thing you'll do is tell me the program is Horses Help and that your former client is named *Gloria."

"That's absolutely right! How did you know?"

"A friend has been trying to get me to volunteer there and has told me about a woman named Gloria who started volunteering with that program many years ago after her husband died. Evidently this Gloria went for counseling at the Casa and the counselor she saw there suggested Gloria try volunteering at Horses Help even though she had never ridden a horse and had no children of her own."

It was my turn to shake my head in wonderment as I pondered God's "sociogram." I had recently retired from the Casa after serving there for nearly 22 years.

While there I had counseled with both Shelly, who had referred Kristen to me, and with Gloria who then spent 17 years with Horses Help. I thus became the second person to suggest to Kristen that she volunteer there. Recently Gloria telephoned to remind me of the circuitous and "coincidental" route by which *she* had connected with me at the Casa.

"Do you remember? A friend told me to call the Casa and ask for an appointment with the psychologist who specialized in grief counseling. Well, when I called the Casa that psychologist did not

---

* Gloria is a pseudonym

have a vacancy and the receptionist offered to either put me on the psychologist's waiting list or arrange for me to see you because you had just had a vacancy open up that day. And so I said, 'I'll try Lynn Leonard,' thinking if it didn't work out, I could always go on the psychologist's waiting list. And the rest is history!"

Gloria continued. "I have *no* idea what made you think to refer a non-horseback riding person to a therapeutic riding program. I *do* know that learning to ride a horse and to help others has transformed my life." As I write this, Gloria and several other horsewomen are developing a therapeutic riding program of their own.

Once again, there may be those who chalk each of these occurrences up to simple happenstance. But seriously, what are the odds that here in the greater metropolitan Phoenix area of 3.6 million souls, Kristen would be referred to me by Shelly, one of the many hundreds of former clients I have seen over the course of 22 years; that Kristen would be a native of my father's and former husband's North Carolina hometown of 10,000; that not only I but also Kristen's friend would refer her to the same therapeutic riding program to which I had referred Gloria, another former client, more than 17 years ago?

> **but those who hope in the LORD will renew their strength. They will soar on wings like eagles; they will run and not grow weary, they will walk and not be faint.**
>
> **Isaiah 40:29-31**

Chapter Seventeen: The Circle Is Unbroken
Greenville, SC—Phoenix, AZ: 1938-2010

No doubt it is a function of my advancing years, but with increasing frequency my mind turns to the joy that filled my heart throughout the seamless weeks of childhood when my parents and I regularly attended Buncombe Street Methodist Church in Greenville. Dad joked, "We're there every time the doors open!"

And so we were. There was a church-centered rhythm to our lives throughout the 1940s and the early 1950s. On Wednesday evenings we joined other church members for supper in the Fellowship Hall. Saturday mornings I attended the children's choir practice conducted by Zelphia Drake. Then on Sunday morning we attended Sunday school followed by church service at 11:00 AM. We then returned for Vesper services in the evening and I also participated in Methodist Youth Fellowship. Throughout the Christmas season the music and beauty of Buncombe Street's sanctuary were all that anyone could dream of. Easter services were gloriously beautiful. In summers I attended Vacation Bible School and reveled in memorizing scripture verses and learning more about God.

Two of my most memorable childhood experiences were those with my mother when she attended a church leadership conference at beautiful Lake Junaluska, the Methodist Retreat Center nestled in the Great Smoky Mountains of North Carolina. In the evening, aboard the *Caroline* out on Lake Junaluska, we sang vesper hymns—our voices blending beautifully and magically amplified by Junaluska's calm and sparkling waters. From the *Caroline* we witnessed God's glorious sunsets and, as the gloaming turned to night, we watched in awe as the 25' tall Junaluska Cross came aglow with its 200 bulbs. Atop its 5' tall granite base, the vision of this cross piercing the inky night and reaching towards God's canopy of stars was a breathtaking sight. "Jubilate" was indeed an appropriate choral celebration at such moments:

Now, on Land and Sea Descending

Now, on land and sea descending,
brings the night its peace profound;
let our vesper hymn be blending
with the holy calm around.
Jubilate! Jubilate! Jubilate! Amen!
Let our vesper hymn be blending
with the holy calm around.

Soon as dies the sunset glory,
stars of heaven shine out above,
telling still the ancient story,
their Creator's changeless love.
Jubilate! Jubilate! Jubilate! Amen!
Telling still the ancient story,
their Creator's changeless love.

Now, our wants and burdens leaving
to God's care who cares for all,
cease we fearing, cease we grieving;
touched by God our burdens fall.
Jubilate! Jubilate! Jubilate! Amen!
Cease we fearing, cease we grieving;
touched by God our burdens fall.

As the darkness deepens o'er us,
lo! eternal stars arise;
hope and faith and love rise glorious,
shining in the Spirit's skies.
Jubilate! Jubilate! Jubilate! Amen!
Hope and faith and love rise glorious,
shining in the Spirit's skies.
Lyrics: Samuel Longfellow 1859. Public Domain.

Back home in Greenville, Buncombe Street Methodist Church continued to be my sanctuary, a place of peace and harmony that I cherished because it filled my need for serenity. My parents had a troubled marriage, one fraught with loud conflict that greatly troubled their only child. At church amid its peace, I could hear myself think. But of far greater importance, through the scripture I learned there and the hymns I sang there, I came to know our Lord and feel His love.

I confess that for far too many years I harbored bitterness towards my parents because I so resented their continual bickering. Today I am happy that in recent years I have at last begun to fully appreciate the very precious gift my parents gave me. No matter how angry and disappointed they were with one another—no matter how weary they were from their work during the war years and the years that followed—they always went to church and took me with them. Knowledge of the triune God they worshipped and shared with me has been my salvation.

As I write these words I can scarcely read them through my tears. What would have become of me had my parents not been churchgoers? What if I had grown up with no awareness of God's Holy Word, without knowledge of His only Son, without the comfort of the Holy Spirit? As lost as I have felt on countless occasions in my lifetime, I cannot imagine that I could have survived without the firm grounding of faith my parents provided.

Yes, my parents were flawed human beings just as are we all. Yet through their efforts—despite their many conflicts—they gave me the most priceless gift of all. Clearly, my faith has not been a matter of coincidence. It was not by chance. My faith was the precious fruit of my parents' faith and their Christian commitment.

As I was reviewing this chapter I watched the *Hour of Power* service from the Crystal Cathedral as I do each Sunday. On July 25, 2010 Dr. Robert H. Schuller's message "Prepare! For Answered Prayer" was a reprise of the sermon he preached many years ago in which he stated, "There are no life spans to prayers." There is no expiration date for prayers. Until hearing Dr. Schuller's message, I had never considered that most of us—while still in our mother's womb—were prayed for by a grandparent, parent, aunt or uncle or family friend. Dr. Schuller described the spiritual universe in which we all live—where we are lovingly embraced by the prayers of friends and family—prayers of those we do know and also by the prayers of many whom we never knew. This perspective filled my heart with gratitude for all who pray not only for the living, but for those who are not yet born.

Thus we are all beneficiaries of the bountiful prayers of our forebears as well as our friends and relatives. Prayer is indeed the unbroken cord that connects us to one another and to God who answers all our prayers in ways that are in our best interest because they are consistent with His perfect plan for us.

My journey has shown me the power of persistent prayer; the wisdom and utmost safety of subordinating my will to God who has in store for me my ultimate good; the importance of trusting God's guidance even when events seem confusing; the necessity of pairing my best effort with my prayers for God's favor and guidance; and finally, the joy that fills my heart when I express my gratitude for all of God's blessings. God does not need my praise. I need the joy that I experience when I praise Him and am grateful to Him.

This backward glance upon my life's journey fills my heart with wonder and deepest gratitude. God has been unfailingly gracious to me throughout my life. His healing touch has enabled me to survive life-threatening and immobilizing depression, to cope with crippling pain and to disprove the dual, discouraging medical prognoses that forecast my inability to walk and to see. My gracious Lord has either removed each boulder that blocked my path or He has guided me to find my way around it. He has provided a companion who assuaged my loneliness—one who is an inspiring example of how to live life faithfully and in accordance with Him from whom all blessings flow. And miracle of miracles, God bridged the span of time and distance that for seven years separated my children and me.

For every mishap that impacted my life—indeed for each misstep that diverted me from His intended path—God has been my GPS, my "God Positioning System." Through His "coincidental" guidance of my life, He has led me upon the path He intended me to follow. He has enabled me to use His healing gifts to benefit those to whom He has guided me.

Each day I awaken immensely grateful that at age 72, I have a mind that is clear of drugs and a body that no longer deals with intractable pain. I am eager to be of service to others who struggle with spiritual, physical or financial challenges because I have something significant to offer them. I pray each night and each morning for God to guide me to connect with those He chooses. And I am confident that His arrangements—His "God winks," or coincidences—will continue to amaze and guide me for the remainder of my earthly journey.

In AA they pose the question, "Is it odd or is it God?" I believe only a loving God could so carefully arrange such elegant and intricate connections as those with which He has guided my life. Thus, with King David I joyfully proclaim:

> **I love the Lord because He has heard**
> **My voice and my supplications.**
> **Because He has inclined His ear to me,**
> **Therefore I will call upon Him as long as**
> **I live. . . .For You have delivered**
> **My soul from death,**
> **My eyes from tears, And my feet**
> **from falling. I will walk before the Lord**
> **In the land of the living.**
>
> **Psalm 116: 1-2, 8-9**

Afterword

Each day our lives are filled with miracles. We can experience the awe and wonder surrounding them only when we open our eyes, our minds, our hearts and our souls to their presence in our lives and to the loving God who placed them there.

As a very small child I recall being overjoyed by the beauty of a rose yet deeply saddened that it could not speak to me. Today I realize the rose did speak to me, albeit in its own language rather than in mine. At that early age I sought to discover the source of the rose's beauty. I began to pluck its petals as I sought that source deep in the center of the rose. Soon the rose's bruised and discarded petals lay at my feet. Having destroyed its beauty, I had discovered nothing of its essence. It's essence remained a mystery.

I vividly recall both the horror and the sadness I experienced the moment I realized my curiosity had destroyed the rose I so adored. This was my earliest and most powerful lesson in learning to accept the "Isness" of life—to allow life's mysteries to unfold naturally—to treasure and embrace life in all its varied forms.

There are universal, infinite mysteries that our finite minds cannot fathom. Yet we can embrace them and give thanks for them. The beauty of the rose is but one such mystery. Today I gladly express my gratitude for the God who has guided me with so many mysterious coincidences. They have served to light the pathway of my earthly journey while providing the comforting assurance of His loving presence.

LCL
July 25, 2010
Lookout Mountain
Phoenix, Arizona

I waited patiently for the Lord to help me,
And he turned to me and heard my cry.
He lifted me out of the pit of despair,
out of the mud and mire.
He set my feet on solid ground
and steadied me as I walked along.
He has given me a new song to sing,
a hymn of praise to our God.
Many will see what He has done for me
and be astounded.
They will put their trust in the Lord.

Psalm 40:1-3 (New Living Translation)

ACKNOWLEDGMENTS

My heartfelt thanks to Sue B. Goldsmith who encouraged me to put God's coincidental guidance of my life in book form so that it might inspire others. *Not By Chance* would not exist were it not for Sue's prompting.

For many years Wilma Lentz, a sister in P.E.O. Chapter D in Phoenix who is an exceptionally gifted writer and voracious reader, encouraged me to write more and to publish my work. Writing is a solitary effort. Being encouraged by a friend possessing Wilma's gifts is a blessing beyond price or praise. Wilma also reviewed the manuscript and her contributions were invaluable.

The careful editorial assistance in Phoenix of two other P.E.O. sisters in Chapter D—Harriet Williams and Mary Wolters—was also invaluable. Each devoted hours to this project, identifying an abundance of errors that would have been most embarrassing had they appeared in print.

WestBow Press provided invaluable assistance beginning with the initial contact and continuing on through to project completion. I especially want to thank: Rodney Clidienst, Colin Boyll, Kristin Bray and Valerie Deem.

Finally, I wish to express long overdue appreciation to Mathilda Canter, Ph.D., for her superb clinical insight and skill, wise guidance and unstinting support. Matty supported me through some devastating chapters in my life, especially during major MS exacerbations, the depressions that accompanied them—and especially following the fateful fall that destroyed my spinal fusion. Matty was truly a gift from God when I was most in need.